From the foreword to *New Beliefs, New Brain*:
"Lisa Wimberger has captured an ageless wisdom and has rephrased it in modern parlance, bringing a new level of approachability to the teachings of our spiritual forebears. And for that I offer up the word *Namaste*."

> — Dr. David Perlmutter, co-author of *Power Up Your Brain: The Neuroscience of Enlightenment*

"Lisa Wimberger has earned the right, through trial by fire, to be regarded as a rising star among meditation teachers. In addition to overcoming her own trauma through meditation techniques, she has helped many others in society who have suffered some of the worst trauma imaginable. No matter where you are in your journey, *New Beliefs, New Brain* will shine a light on your path."

> — Marianne Williamson, author of *A Return to Love, Everyday Grace*, and *A Course in Weight Loss*

"Lisa Wimberger is the perfect blend of intellect, storyteller, and gifted teacher. She utilizes her passion and knowledge of meditation to give us all tools that can assist us in becoming more centered and to transcend old ways of being that no longer serve. I believe *New Beliefs, New Brain* will support many people on the road to health."

> — Cynthia James, author of *What Will Set You Free* and *Revealing Your Extraordinary Essence*

"*New Beliefs, New Brain* shows us how to overcome self-imposed limitations, clearly explaining how we can take charge of our lives through focused intentions and persistence. Drawing on her own recovery from life-threatening traumatic experiences, Lisa Wimberger offers an easy and effective combination of theory and practical methods on how to lead a creative and stress-free life."

> — Dale E. Graff, physicist and author of *River Dreams* and *Tracks in the Psychic Wilderness*, former director of project STARGATE, the military psychic remote viewing program

"New Beliefs, New Brain is a breakthrough doorway to the new intersection of science, shamanism, and peak consciousness performance. With specific recommendations for nutrition, behavioral programs, useful belief systems, and more, Lisa Wimberger illuminates the scientific and personal paths that optimize human performance, evolution, and potential in a completely new way."

> — Norman Katz, PhD, Assistant Clinical Professor, UNM Medical School 1985-1999. Founder, Erickson Institute of Hypnosis and Behavioral Sciences of New Mexico

"New Beliefs, New Brain is not only inspiration on many levels but also a practical manual for examining the personal stories that either empower us or limit our ability to thrive and heal. Combining brain research with anecdotes from her life that illustrate how the brain works, Lisa Wimberger illustrates that the brain can and does grow and change throughout our lives."

> — LD Thompson, author of *The Message: A Guide to Being Human*

"The mind is a terrible thing. In this new book, Lisa Wimberger helps you escape it. *New Beliefs New Brain* is a practical, grounded, and highly uplifting tool for helping you leave the orbit of everyday thinking and experience a profound level of peace and well-being—no drugs or lobotomies required. How great is that?"

> — John Marshall Roberts, author of *Igniting Inspiration: A Persuasion Manual for Visionaries*

NEW BELIEFS
BELIEFS

FREE YOURSELF FROM STRESS AND FEAR

NEW
BRAIN

LISA WIMBERGER

DIVINE
ARTS

Published by DIVINE ARTS
DivineArtsMedia.com

An imprint of Michael Wiese Productions
12400 Ventura Blvd. # 1111
Studio City, CA 91604
(818) 379-8799, (818) 986-3408 (Fax)
www.mwp.com

Cover design by Johnny Ink www.johnnyink.com
Copyediting by Andrew Beierle
Book layout by Gina Mansfield Design

Printed by McNaughton & Gunn, Inc., Saline, Michigan
Manufactured in the United States of America

Library of Congress Cataloging-in-Publication Data

Wimberger, Lisa, 1969-
  New beliefs, new brain : free yourself from stress and fear / Lisa Wimberger.
      p. cm.
   Summary: "Stress is a silent killer. New Beliefs, New Brain shares methods for
healing the negative impacts of stress and fear that many police and firefighters rely
on to stay sharp on the job and in life -- "first responders" have the MOST stressful
jobs! Combining her personal experiences with an effective and easy-to-understand
approach, Lisa Wimberger teaches powerful meditation practices that will improve the
mental and emotional quality of life for those who are suffering. These techniques can
be used at any time to turn back the body's clock, regenerate the mind, break negative
patterns, and heal emotional wounds"-- Provided by publisher.
   ISBN 978-1-61125-013-8 (pbk.)
   1. Meditation--Therapeutic use. 2. Meditation--Health aspects. I. Title.
   RC489.M43W56 2012
   615.8'528--dc23
                                    2012017727

Printed on Recycled Stock

DEDICATION

γ

With respect to my brother, Eric—a most unsuspecting teacher.

ACKNOWLEDGEMENTS

How does one begin to thank all of those who've helped her on her journey? This is, by far, the most difficult part to write, as I fear I may forget to give enough thanks. In my humble attempt to recognize all those who've contributed to this work, I must begin with my husband, Gilly, and my daughter, Havana, who are the most patient and loving beings I could have wished for. My parents and brothers played a huge part in this lifelong journey, setting the stage for all of this. I have the most amazing support community of friends who give me so much love and belief that it's almost impossible to fail at anything. I am deeply grateful for all of this.

Specifically, I want to thank Michael Wiese, Manny Otto, and everyone at Divine Arts Media for seeing something of value in my story. I am grateful to Amber Taufen for her consistent, clear, and continued support of my trauma work. I have had so many influences along the way that seem integral to my development that I couldn't possibly fit them all here. So my deepest thanks for all of the great teachers in my life.

Mostly, I am thanking you. Although you might be faceless to me, you are truly the reason I do what I do.

TABLE OF CONTENTS

FOREWORD

Dr. David Perlmutter

Scientific historians generally credit the American psychologist and philosopher William James with the first descriptions of what we now refer to as *neuroplasticity*, the brain's ability to change and reorganize itself both structurally and functionally. In his landmark text, *The Principles of Psychology* (1890), James wrote, "Organic matter, especially nervous tissue, seems endowed with a very extraordinary degree of plasticity." His views ran counter to the prevailing view that the brain was basically static and unchanging as proposed by the Spanish histologist Ramón y Cajal, who stated "Once the development was ended, the founts of growth and regeneration of the axons and dendrites dried up irrevocably. In the adult centers, the nerve paths are something fixed, ended, and immutable. Everything may die, nothing may be regenerated. It is for the science of the future to change, if possible, this harsh decree."

Fortunately, the challenge for science was indeed met, with modern research discounting the deterministic dictum of Ramón y Cajal and validating the idea of the ever-changing brain that James proposed.

Later researchers not only demonstrated that the human brain remains in a dynamic state of renovation, but moreover, science validated the contention that the changes that each of our brains will experience are dictated by the very choices we make in terms of the direction of our thoughts, interests, and pursuits. Indeed, as Buddha stated, "The mind is everything. What you think you become." Or as Gandhi said, "We are the product of what we think. What we think, we become."

We now have powerful scientific validation for what at first blush may have appeared to be almost poetic language from our deeply regarded spiritual leaders.

So more recently, when His Holiness the Dalai Lama counseled that "The brain we develop reflects the life we lead," it's important to understand that his statement reflects not only a call for us to live a life of compassion based on his spiritual pursuits, but that in addition these words are a reflection of his deep understanding of modern neuroscience.

The idea that our brains are malleable and that each of us is the steward of that change is both compelling and empowering. And it is in this setting of limitless opportunity that *New Beliefs, New Brain: Free Yourself from Stress and Fear* is presented.

In the pages that follow, Lisa Wimberger lovingly describes her time-proven techniques allowing the reader to literally reconfigure his or her brain from a functional perspective, granting each of us the opportunity to more fully experience the joy and compassion of the human experience while relinquishing our ties to previous dysfunctional and destabilizing thought processes. Transformation, especially when dedicated to these lofty goals, isn't necessarily an easy process. But you absolutely can and will make the changes you so desperately seek if you dedicate yourself to the techniques so skillfully refined in this text.

Lisa has captured an ageless wisdom and has rephrased it in modern parlance, bringing a new level of approachability to the teachings of our spiritual forebears. And for that I offer up the word *Namaste*.

David Perlmutter, MD, FACN, ABIHM

www.DrPerlmutter.com

INTRODUCTION

Every story has a beginning, the point from which all action, perception, and exploration unfolds. Each story we read or tell ourselves holds within it the potential for transformation, learning, and healing. We can each recall a moment in time from which a certain series of our life's events evolved. Have you ever heard yourself say, "It all started when . . . " or "I remember the first time I . . . " But this presupposes one thing—that the initial story itself is a representation of reality. We'd all like to believe that our life's history is based on something real rather than illusion. But the truth is we tell ourselves stories every minute of every day—stories of who we are, who we've been, and who we should be. Those stories drift out from us, spreading their seeds to take root and create a history into which we anchor. When the mind tells us a story, we believe it. But what if the story you're telling yourself right now is the driving force behind your pain, stress, and fear? What would you do differently?

We are all healers—some of us healers of ourselves, some of us healers of others. Some of us are dormant, believing we have no ability to tap into this phenomenon of emotional, mental, physical, and spiritual healing. Some of us are awakening to our own inherent abilities of transformation. Others are steeped in the practice of healing all we can. Where you start matters little to your own ability to fully recognize and awaken innate healing potential in whatever time you have left in your body.

Your clock is ticking.

My intention in writing *New Beliefs, New Brain: Free Yourself from Stress and Fear* is to connect with you in as intimate and real a way as the written word allows—to share with you some extremely real and powerful concepts that shaped my clients' and my life experiences (our self-told stories) into tools for stress relief, healing, and transformation. The techniques presented in this book are the ammunition against my darkest drives, my armor against the layers of negativity and disease the world throws me, and my strategy for transformation and healing. I believe these tools belong in your cache of coping mechanisms, because you can't have too many healthy ways of making sense of the world and your purpose in it. The tools I present to you come from a variety of disciplines and backgrounds, many of which were taught to me under extremely different pretenses. I have culled some of the simplest—yet most powerful—procedures and presented them here for you. Although some of what I share comes from many of my teachers, I have found a way to make these techniques my own—and you will too.

Our lifespan is merely a blip on a screen of vast earth and space history. We have a choice in how we want to spend that precious time. Some of us yield to pain, punishment, stress, and anxiety; others fight hard to choose joy, love, and compassion. Yes, sometimes we must fight our own selves to access joy. Still, most of us don't even realize it's a choice at all. I urge you to get out of your own way and recognize your own potential and power to choose so that you may experience the master within you— that part of you that no longer surrenders to your negative beliefs or destructive self-talk. Albert Einstein said, "We have to do the best we can. This is our sacred human responsibility." I am speaking directly to you as I tell you that I am here to do the best I can; I am here to help—not as a therapist, psychologist, psychotherapist, minister, doctor, or scientist. I am none of those things. Nor am I pious, perfect, squeaky clean, noble, innocent, correct, omniscient, irrefutable, or infallible. I know firsthand what it's like to be embarrassingly wrong, sophomorically opinionated, egotistically grandiose, smugly condescending, grossly miscalculating, deceitful, and utterly headed for disaster. It's from this place that I am here to help, simply as a fellow human who stumbles along the way, but one who is also blessed by having learned some amazing navigation techniques that have literally saved my life and preserved my sanity. It is not my intention to have you place this book on the shelf in some category marked "interesting yet impractical motivational books." My goal is to offer you a rich context, strong examples, practical exercises, realistic application, and direct experience—to offer you a guide to freeing yourself from stress and fear. On some level we are each our own nemesis, but you deserve to know you are also the victor.

I believe, as science and our DNA shows, that we are all much more similar than we are different. From that platform, I look at us as brothers and sisters. As an integral part of our human family, it is my purpose on this planet to reach out my hand to those who struggle. Where would I be if others hadn't offered me help or supported me when I needed it? Whether the struggle is to awaken healing abilities, make ends meet, deal with an ugly work situation, rear children with patience, muscle through depression, or even contemplate suicide—there is no situation outside our collective human experience that excuses me from doing what I can, where I can.

Like you, I'm just a participant in this life journey—adept in some things, novice in many, expert in few. To cut to the chase so we may get on with our connection, I'll note some of my experience so your logic mind can judge whether or not I have anything to offer you. After that critical point, if you decide I have nothing to offer, then you can quietly close these pages and continue your path. If your judgment of my experience deems it valuable, then you can get on with the dance your right and left brain is about to do as we connect, face fears, make choices, and learn how to rewrite our stories together—one page at a time.

A LINEAR HISTORY

I began self-hypnosis and my meditation practice at age twelve, after my college-aged brother taught me a technique he learned from a professor. I was a fish to water. Nothing had ever been so natural. My commitment to daily meditation was effortless. I never once thought to question why I was meditating twice a day; I simply did it. It felt good. It felt right. It gave me a buzz I loved but didn't quite understand. This is neither the time nor place to detail those experiences, but suffice it to say an entire book can, and likely will, be written just on my meditation experiences alone—some of them extremely pragmatic and some of them absolutely otherworldly.

As a young teenager, I voraciously read anything I could get my hands on to help explain the invisible forces and benefits behind meditation and metaphysics. I read about chakras, Buddhism, breath work, meditation, extrasensory perception, hypnosis, super-power memory, shamanic journeys, and much more. My reading informed my practice; my practice often informed me and sometimes confused me just as much—but I never stopped.

While my peers experimented with drugs in junior high school and high school, I was clean, sober, and quite adept at escaping reality through my own meditations and fantasy. By the time I'd finished high school I'd accumulated a rich fantasy life which seemed to bleed its intensity into my day-to-day world. Meditation was my bedfellow, my dream journals were my secret friends, and my metaphysical experiences were my fuel. I kept this rich world secret from those close to me, as I was afraid of disapproval. I had an infinite number of questions and few answers at this time in my life.

In college I first majored in engineering, as science fascinated me. I also attribute that choice to having been raised in a very pragmatic family in which many of my male role models were also engineers. Yet two years later I became a literature major, trying to balance my ability to live in my left brain some of the time and in my right brain the rest of the time. Each perspective seduced me uniquely.

I graduated college with a bachelor's of English and a masters in education and literature. So much for passing calculus 3 and differential equations! I went on to become a middle school and high school teacher—only to find I was so ill-equipped to deal with the human side of teaching that within two weeks of embarking on my new career I swore at the students in class, then went home with stress, tension headaches, depression, uncontrollable anger, and a sense of hopelessness. This was odd to me, as I had experienced some intense physical trauma up to this point: blinded twice, hit by lightning, experienced seizures and flat-lined on numerous occasions. I will share more about that in later chapters. I already viewed myself as a warrior, a tough New Yorker, so dealing with human interaction (I thought) was supposed to be easy. It was humbling to have a room full of thirteen-year-old students stare at me apathetically as I slipped over the edge. Try standing in front of a group of teenagers sometime. It's humbling. I had never felt so naked.

In response to my career complaints and disillusionment I was given this advice: *If you enjoy even ten percent of your job, consider yourself lucky.* The advice came from a well-meaning place, but how was a statement of such grim disposition supposed to make me feel better? Each day that I arrived at my classroom the teacher across the hall called out a number instead of "good morning." This perplexed me. The numbers descended consecutively every day. After a week of this I finally asked what it all meant. He told me it was the number of days left until his retirement in three years. I began to see that people really lived like that—in a state of total compromise, stress, and pain acceptance. I began to look around at my colleagues in fear that I'd end up as cynical and exhausted as they were. Was that what it was like to be in the real world—that you were lucky if you enjoyed ten percent of your life? That the only positive thing you could focus on is a day, years into the future, at which point all of this misery would end? I could not accept that reality. There had to be a better way. I was accused over and over by those I loved of having my head in the sand and seeing through rose-colored glasses—or as a poet friend of mine likes to say, "grace-tainted lenses." It was their euphemistic way of calling me naïve, as they truly believed they knew the truth of how things *really* were. (I would later come to know that looking through rose-colored glasses was one of the greatest and most powerful gifts I'd been given.)

Handling my stress became paramount as I felt my career integrity slipping fast. Up to this point I had done self-hypnosis, lucid dreaming, chakra meditations, shamanic journeys, and dream journaling. It was here that I began studying Ascension meditation with Ishaya monks. I first began my studies of Ascension in Brooklyn at the home of a friend. Weekend workshops soon filled my time as I continued my studies with the Ishayas, when I could, for about four years. The experiences were rich and visceral. I never tired of learning new ways to dive into my mind's ability to unravel worlds within worlds and extrapolate information that always seemed to directly apply to what I was going through. My Ascension practice changed absolutely *everything* in my career. I got rid of my headaches and depression in a matter of days with the new techniques I learned. Within weeks, I began to see something I never expected: The worst, most damaged children no longer misbehaved in my class. For just forty-five minutes of their day, they seemed to blossom in a space where I no longer judged them. Don't misunderstand—I was strict and there were consequences for poor behavior, but the personal judgment that previously defined our interactions disappeared as I began to understand and release my own pain more deeply and get a handle on my stress. The children and I thrived.

I remember the most profound example of this ripple effect. A student—the worst in my class and one I absolutely dreaded interacting with—did something one day that completely dumbfounded me. He got up in the middle of the lesson, walked calmly to the front of the room with his text book in hand, wound up and slammed the girl in the front seat right across the back of the head while calling her *"nigger."* Yes, this was really seventh grade in New York. My education never once taught me ways to deal with *this* reality. The student was in severe pain and totally devastated. After tending to her, I took the boy out in the hall with the real desire to hurt him. It took all of my efforts to just breathe. My face was red, my heart pounding, my hands clenched, and my thoughts hateful. Once face-to-face, I just took thirty seconds to breathe quietly and silently repeat one of the mantras I'd learned through Ascension. In that short time, a miracle occurred. He asked me why I wasn't yelling at him, why I wasn't telling him he was worthless. My answer was the truth: I simply did not understand who or what he was, and I couldn't communicate with him until I did. His eyes shifted and welled up with tears. He asked me if I actually cared to know who he was. I asked him to help *me* help *him.* He stayed after school that day and I found out his horrific life story. He was the only child of a single mother who worked multiple jobs. She was a provider but a negligent nurturer. On a visit one day from social services, the only thing they found in the kitchen was cat food. He had been coming home from school each day to an empty, roach-infested house, feeding himself cat food for dinner, and going to bed alone. He stole other children's lunch money in order to buy his own lunch, as that was the only human food he knew he'd eat all day. He was a total outcast. He was twelve and had been functioning like this most of his life. My heart broke. After that interaction, he never once misbehaved in my class, and he apologized to the girl. He often stayed after school to be with me because it was a nightmare being at home. He was a broken little boy who wanted to break everyone else. It was that initial moment of breath I learned from my Ascension meditations that opened my eyes to the powerful force of change I could be for myself and others in the world. Could a few seconds of nonjudgement really open the doors to profound connection?

As stress dissipated from my life, I found a way to relate and teach with passion. I began to see that important guidance and information really lived in the layers of my stories. It is this vast depth of stress-management and interoception (awareness of stimuli originating from one's internal state) I am eager to help you tap into. It takes no special skill, no previous insight, and no magical fairy dust. It simply takes your willingness and some of the amazing processes I share in this book.

By the time I was twenty-eight, I had been meditating regularly for sixteen years—yet I still felt it would take a lifetime to understand the power of what I was doing. To the best of my recollection, I was still a hot-headed, opinionated, sometimes violent, reactionary, and critical person—not transcendent by any stretch of my own definitions. I recall more than a few incidents of intense anger that caused me to see red, break glass, punch holes in walls, smack faces, and scream like a banshee. I was unclear about the depths from which this rage boiled at times. I can only hope those on the other end of the experiences have found ways to forgive me.

The more I discovered about myself, the more I felt life was a vast mystery hinting at galaxies of information of which I only had the smallest glimpse. I went on to work in the corporate world, getting certifications in different human behavior modalities, coaching and mentoring management teams, and creating and delivering people skills under whatever context I was asked: Meyers-Briggs assessments, performance improvement, training and development, stress management, daily coaching, and more. The names are irrelevant; I was employed to look at human behavior and find a way to improve it. Most of my academic training was behavior-based, but from personal experience I knew there was a powerful emotional, mental, and spiritual component informing all of my actions. I believed I should pursue deeper training in these other areas. I enrolled to study the techniques of the Berkeley Psychic Institute at a school in Denver. The curriculum was presented under the context of psychic awareness. I had experienced psychic awareness most of my life and this seemed to fit a purpose I thought I had. Shortly after the commencement of my training, I realized that these same techniques had far greater implications—they were revolutionary in terms of stress management and trauma release. I completed two-and-a-half years of psychic awareness training and another year-and-a-half of postgraduate studies. After four years of intensive study in these meditational methods I finally felt equipped to bring some of what I knew out to the world. And after working with the public for a few years, I strengthened my own tool kit by obtaining a certification in the Foundations of NeuroLeadership, which involved a much deeper understanding of the brain's neurological landscape. I have spent many thousands of dollars on my education and pursuit of stress and trauma relief, but I don't feel you should have to. I believe it is your right to have these techniques at your disposal.

I want to mention here that I define the term meditation very broadly; so many subset skills have grown out of my practice that I find it difficult to draw lines. For me, meditation includes affirmations, mantras, mindfulness, no thought, deep breathing, visualization, music, yoga, dance, astral projection, remote viewing, lucid dreaming, psychic awareness, channeling, and more. You have the freedom to define meditation any way you'd like. But for the sake of common ground, I propose that meditation *is a method of intentional thought designed to give one internal and external awareness capabilities—an experience of interoception.*

Since 2007, I have been formally teaching meditation for all levels of trauma release, running meditation groups and workshops, facilitating Neurosculpting® trainings (a modality I created), and teaching stress-management to law-enforcement agencies, corporations, and state and municipal agencies. My private clients range from the average person looking for intuitive information or stress-management tips to officers with PTSD contemplating suicide.

I have taken some of the most practical methods that worked with all of my clients and presented them here for you, along with some preliminary exercises to help prepare you for the later techniques. Part I is intended to help you identify the stories you may be telling yourself which perpetuate stressful responses to the world around you—the stories that prime you to lose your battle. Part II is a deep dive into specific meditations I use with most (if not all) of my clients. Part III includes case studies ranging from individuals who use these tools for everyday balance to individuals who have used these tools to save their own lives.

If you choose to approach it this way, then what you're holding in your hands is a workbook designed to prime you for easy stress management and life-healing transformation. I recommend doing each exercise in a dedicated journal before moving on to the following chapters. You also have the option to treat this book as an informational read and simply skip the exercises. You can come back to them any time you want for a deeper experience of this material.

To be clear: If you are under the care of a physician, therapist, or counselor, then please *do not* use this book as a reason to interrupt or modify your care in any way. Additionally, if you are not under the care of a professional and you feel you need to be, *do not* use this book as a reason to delay getting help. All of these techniques are intended to be used in conjunction with, not in lieu of, licensed professional mental health services. Additionally, there is no religious or political dogma associated with the exercises presented. I feel no need to have you validate my spiritual practice, nor do I feel a need to change or influence yours. Masters come in all beliefs, shapes, and sizes.

My time is thin as a mother, wife, stress-management and meditation practitioner, friend, musician, and dancer. So when I posed the question *how can I help more?* the answer came: through the written word. Life is speeding up, globalizing, concentrating, and potentializing. I no longer feel the need to have my life be perfect before I share what I know. In fact, I will never share from a place of perfection because I've learned that is an illusion. I am sharing with you now, from a place of integrity, knowing that every single thing I say in this book has truly shaped my life's experiences for the better.

I may never meet you, yet my life's work commits me to *your* healing. In the spirit of honoring Einstein and living up to my sacred human responsibility, I go back to the principle of doing what I can, where I can. I'll start here, where I can, and tell you that I believe in YOU . . . but I don't believe in your stories.

So what exactly are those stories?

PART I

DISCOVERING
YOUR STORIES

Chapter I

STORYTELLER MIND

In spite of modern dependence on technology and industry, in my opinion, we are still products of folklore tradition. Although we may no longer take comfort sharing tribal stories around campfires to define who we are, our minds fervently uphold that human tradition. We tell ourselves stories all the time. In a tribal society, this memorializes cultural identity and unifies individuals. A tribal identity predicts the success of the group as a function of how well the individuals work together. But for those of us who function as individuals competing in a survival-of-the-fittest paradigm, our stories form somewhat in isolation and in reaction to the world around us. We develop a sense of ourselves through repetitive internal thoughts, internally processed experiences, and a left brain that loves to fill in gaps of fact with a narrative to make sense of who we are.

As the world has sped up and become more efficient, we have the luxury of time in which to think, reflect, ponder, stew, and even fester. How I define me derives from a story I constantly tell myself, and the premise is this: *I am a unique individual separate from "you."* To me, *this* is our modern folklore. It identifies us as individuals separate from tribe. And while this may have social benefits not discussed here, it also sanctions our solitary internal stories as the authority of our identities. We are now arriving at theories of biological tribe mentality, noticing that our cells, minds, and bodies exist in an ever-dynamic group dance. However, the rest of our lives haven't quite embraced these notions. If our individual perspectives dictate who we are, and we define ourselves as separate from (or in competition with) the rest of *you*, then challenge, territorialism, and threat, rather than ease, permeates all of our interactions. Can you sense the "us and them" dilemma?

MASTER STORYTELLER

When the mind tells us a story, we believe it. Our brains are the greatest of all bards—*the* master storytellers. Each moment, action, and experience filters through our colored beliefs, which grow out of our environment, history, biology, and nurturing. Every word, gesture, and action translates through *my* perception of the world. From *my* space, it's easy to minimize, assume, misread, or negate another person's intention. Each action of every individual I encounter passes through *my* lens before I even interact with it on a conscious level. For example: If my perception is that the world is dangerous and people are not to be trusted, how might I perceive new neighbors who stare at my house whenever I come and go? I might think they were scoping my house or that they were rudely nosey. Would I perceive their same actions differently if my filter was one of trust and tribal mentality? I might then think that they were trying to make eye contact as an excuse to get my attention or meet me. Or think about this: If my lens was one that believed all men let me down, then how would I perceive those times when my husband forgot one item on the grocery list? Wouldn't I be predisposed to frustration and annoyance and possibly adopt a condescending attitude as I said something like, "I knew you'd forget the *one* thing I needed!" Have you heard yourself use the "I knew you'd . . . " statement with a loved one before? I translate that statement this way: What you're *really* saying is you believed the worst about them all along, and you were simply waiting for them to make a mistake and validate that belief. How much of your loved ones' best behavior have you missed? How much of your own best behavior has been missed by others?

Friend or Foe, a Powerful Delusion

Here's a much starker example that Dr. Kevin Gilmartin, a well-respected behavioral psychologist and former police officer, uses in his police trainings. He asks officers to call out their first response to the term "Boy Scout leader." You might be surprised to know that the majority of immediate, uncensored answers are *"pedophile."* I have seen this to be consistent with over seven hundred officers I've taught (including some FBI, Secret Service, Military, and Homeland Security personnel). Obviously, the majority of Boy Scout leaders are amazing individuals devoted to teaching empowering skills to our children. However, if you were, or are, an officer, then the reality of your professional interactions with Boy Scout leaders would likely be because you were arresting them, investigating allegations, or interrogating them. This experience begins to shape a perception, which then drives an undercurrent of belief. Their work-related world view begins to replace their personal world view. At one point in time, they probably didn't believe Boy Scout leaders were pedophiles; however, that belief gets chipped away and replaced with a new one that's validated over and over again by their profession. Even though it's likely that fewer than one percent of all Boy Scout leaders are pedophiles, a cop will easily adopt this view as the truth that overrides their former belief. When an officer returns home from work at the end of the day, he doesn't magically begin to trust all Boy Scout leaders. Instead, he maintains a skewed, but validated, work-related world view.

We unknowingly participate in this one-sided ego validation: **My** *perception, validated by the tiniest sliver of life's experience, is the **true** perception.* This belief also happens to be man's most powerful delusion.

Our stories cover life's full spectrum. What exactly are these stories?

I am ugly.

I am fat.

Our environment is dangerous.

I am not as good as . . .

I am better than . . .

I must prove myself.

I am entitled to . . .

I can't because . . .

No pain, no gain.

You only have yourself to rely on.

Losing is bad.

Winning is good.

You always let me down.

You are not as good as . . .

I'll never . . .

They shouldn't because . . .

. . . and on and on.

Are you familiar with any of these?

MY STORY

We each have our own list of stories defining our role in this world. One of my childhood stories was that I wasn't tall enough. I was a tiny girl—half the weight and size of my peers. I weighed thirty-four pounds in third grade—as much as my daughter weighed when she was four! It was the spring concert, and I was so proud to wear my new polyester skirt and wedge heels. My mother labored with the hot comb to somewhat smooth out my fuzzy curls. I wanted my hair shiny like Dorothy Hamill's—it was the seventies. Just before the show, the music teacher separated me from my classmates and placed me in the front line with the first graders, so we'd look uniform. Rationale barely consoled my complete embarrassment and sense of isolation. I could hardly sing or hold back the tears. I prayed for the concert to end. My friends had one another for comfort up there on the third tier. I had no one. I believed my physicality equaled isolation. At that age I had no academic understanding that rejection and isolation are wired into the brain as powerfully as physical pain, but I sure could feel it.

My size dictated many logistical issues in my life, such as the inability to go on the amusement park rides with my friends or the constant assumption that I was someone's little sister. Over the years, I grew my personality to overcompensate for my stature. I would later spend lots of energy finding ways to be seen through argumentative debate, obnoxious analysis, and outright confrontation—*you'll see me now!* I waited on every word, ready to pounce on the most innocent of mistakes. The "I knew you'd . . ." statement had a front row seat in my vernacular. Once, in order to prove my mother spoke with poor grammar, I secretly recorded her phone conversation from the next room on a tape recorder and played it back for her. I was very young then, and I must have come across as a smug and condescending little child. My parents affectionately joked that I should be a lawyer. (No offense to lawyers intended.)

I mourned as friends grew into young women years before I would. My pit-bull stance and sense of overcompensation thickened and curdled into a stubborn defense of what a woman "should" be. Women should be valued for intellect and wit, *not* their bodies. I both envied and hated my curvaceous friends. I didn't often need new clothes, as the girls in the neighborhood gave me their hand-me-downs years after they had worn them. Eventually, I got my own curves and thought I was doing just fine . . . until one day in my late twenties I realized my childhood story was still there, insidiously informing my everyday.

While visiting my parents back home, my partner cheated on me in my house . . . in my bed.

The other woman was my polar opposite: more than six feet tall, big breasts, polished face and nails, and expensive dyed, straight hair. The affair tortured my ego. I was sick to my stomach often, depressed, and I didn't want to leave the house—seemingly because the relationship trust had been violated. I was grieving the relationship, right? But I had not been a model of perfect trust at all times. Righteousness masked the real source of my torture. My childhood story—no longer content to be an incessantly whispering narrator—rose up, took a deep breath, and proclaimed itself boldly. In talking with a friend, I heard myself say, "His mistress is everything I'm not, she looks like a *real* woman." Ah, the bandage ripped off. Finally, the source of torture was a revelation I'd forever be thankful for, as I then focused on the "real" healing: redefining my sense of what it meant to be a real woman. I realized my definition of womanhood was created from my overcompensation for what I lacked. This is a sad, but commonplace, reality for most of us. We define ourselves by overcompensating for what we lack, rather than basking in our inherent strengths.

Interestingly, the brain has about 100 billion neurons. Within that complex network, there are five times as many neuron maps associated with and allocated to identifying negative stories rather than positive stories. It's an easy default to focus on what's wrong rather than what's right. So the sage advice of focusing on the positive just isn't that easy sometimes.

YOU, THE GLUE

But why did my childhood story carry so much weight, so many years later? To what lengths would my mind go to hold on to negative stories that caused me stress and pain? To what could I attribute the sticking power of this story as it seemed to run as a narrative for twenty-eight years? The clues to healing only came through my inward navigation of my own mind-body relationship. My story of stature was one of a myriad stories painting my personality, behaviors, and preferences. How many times does insult, disregard, judgment, or dismissal pain you? Can you say for sure you know the reasons behind your pain? I know this amazing Cherokee proverb that goes something like this:

An old Cherokee told his grandson that a battle goes on inside each of us. The battle is between two wolves. One wolf is evil. It has anger, envy, jealousy, sorrow, regret, greed, arrogance, self-pity, guilt, resentment, inferiority, lies, false pride, superiority, and ego. The other wolf is good. It has joy, peace, love, hope, serenity, humility, kindness, benevolence, empathy, generosity, truth, compassion, and faith.

The grandson thought about it for a minute and then asked his grandfather, "Which one wins?" The old Cherokee simply replied, "The one you feed."

If our stories control our personalities, behaviors and preferences, then who controls the stories? Who (and what) are you feeding? I have found the answer is so simple that no one really wants to hear it.

YOU.

I will say it again, just so you can't gloss over it: YOU are the answer.

It is exactly at this point that every meditation training I ever attended and every workshop I ever taught has the potential to derail as individuals slam on the brakes, protest with raised fists, and bark at this inane supposition.

How could I be the answer?

Believe me when I tell you that knowing we are *truly* in control of our own stories is a liberating idea *if* you are ready to own it. If you are not, then it can be a dark and brutal spiral back into denial, victim mentality, and pain deferral. This is also the exact point at which a debate or conversation becomes derisive argument as individuals revert to blame instead of ownership. I have seen individuals shut down instantly as they realize they must take responsibility for changing their stories. Some of you healthy skeptics are using a lot of mental energy right now creating and finding reasons why it's impossible to change some of your stories. Good news—you don't have to believe *me*. Fortunately, science proves you have this ability. Neuroplasticity proves we can change our stories, rewire our defaults, and create new perspectives *at will*—YOUR will.

You might be wondering what exactly I mean by YOUR will. Is it as simple as willing a bad situation to feel good or making false and contradictory statements like *Today is great!* when it really is terrible? For some, it is not as simple as one-line affirmations; for others, it is. Remember that insecure and depressed character on the '90s *Saturday Night Live* episodes named Stuart Smalley? He stood in front of a mirror with a cardigan on and repeated over and over, "I'm good enough, I'm smart enough, and gosh darn it, people like me." Like so many of us who've tried using affirmations, it can become a mockery if one has no will to believe it. Growing up in New York gifted me with an edge at an early age—it made me tenacious and simultaneously sarcastic and skeptical. It's a miracle I was so open to meditation at all. I remember trying affirmations and thinking they were totally useless. Later I learned they were not, but without the will to believe what I was saying to myself it was difficult to reap the benefits. This is why the tool kit I present to you later in the book is so helpful. It helps you articulate your will by detailing practical steps which prime your brain, making your new story more plausible. You'll learn how to get out of your own way in much the same way I learned.

I am reminded often of a creation story Alan Watts wrote about in *The Book*. To paraphrase, the idea was that the Supreme Being, omniscient and omnipresent, wanted to have an experience of itself. In order to do this, it had to experience "other." It then created man and put pieces of itself inside each of us, so that when it looked upon another, it could recognize itself in each of us—like looking in a mirror. But in this story, it hid so well that it forgot it was playing hide-and-seek, and it began to believe that each of us is separate, individual, and basically alone. This became our truth and our delusion.

So how do you get out of your own way? You remember you're playing a game and recognize that the truth is a lie!

Exercise 1: Know Thyself
The purpose of this exercise is to become familiar with some of your identity perceptions. Keep this list because you will work with it again in later exercises in both Parts I and II. My dear friend and hypnotherapist Teddy Rachlin helped me compose this exercise.

Part 1: Find some alone time in a comfortable place that makes you feel little pressure. This might be your favorite room in the house or maybe an outside location. It's not recommended you do this at work or with others. In a journal that you will continue to use throughout this book, list as many uncensored **I AM** statements as possible. You may take breaks and come back to this list at various points, but try to complete this exercise before proceeding to Chapter 2. Examples: I am strong, I am easily angered, I am a martyr, I am detail oriented, etc. It is important for you not to censor out the ones you believe to be negative descriptions. Include both negative and positive statements. Rely on your own ideas of who you are instead of others' descriptions of you.

Take a short break or a few minutes to yourself before continuing to the next part of this exercise.

Part 2: Once you've completed the list, use a clean sheet in your journal to create two columns. Title the first column **Aspects of Myself I Easily Accept** and the second column **Aspects of Myself I Resist and Hope to Change.** Go back to the **I AM** list from the first part of this exercise and categorize all of your written statements into these two columns. Without judgment, simply notice the percentage of **I AM** statements you accept easily versus the amount you resist. Resistance to our own self-definitions sets up an internal state of conflict—in other words, a state of stress!

Aspects of myself I easily accept	Aspects of myself I resist and hope to change
I am organized	I am hot-headed
I am punctual	I am reactionary
I am ...	I am ...

Chapter 2

TRUTH AS A CONSPIRACY:
THE SECRET ALLIANCE BETWEEN OUR RIGHT AND LEFT BRAINS

"If the facts don't fit the theory, change the facts."

"Reality is merely an illusion, albeit a persistent one."

~ Albert Einstein

David Eagleman, neuroscientist at Baylor College of Medicine, says in his book *Incognito: Secret Lives of the Brain* that the brain functions like a democracy—where different factions make overlapping decisions then battle it out until a dominating opinion wins and thus controls and directs behavior. Parallel processing, where items get processed simultaneously in different areas, is a much quicker and energy-efficient way to deal with data. I'm simplifying a great deal, but accredited to this type of system is our amazing ability to evolve, adapt, and make exponential leaps in logic, inspiration, and creation. This type of democratic brain system takes competing ideas, thoughts, or realities and entertains them simultaneously in an active debate between multiple parts of the brain. Whichever part wins the particular debate seems to be the story we end up identifying as our truth or reality. And—as in any debate—neither side is wrong; one simply gets backed by a bit more momentum and substantiation, tipping the scales in its favor. It is exactly this way with our own truths.

We have conflicting truths running concurrently all the time in our brains. Let's say it's a beautiful day and you decide you want to go hiking. Some of your conflicting truths might be: *It's dangerous to be hiking*

alone in the woods versus *I am resourceful and independent.* In the case of this conflict, if the former truth won you might make a decision to ask someone
else to go hiking with you—or you might decide not to go hiking at all.
If the latter won, you might decide to go by yourself and deal with the
risk. Now think about this truth debate: *Money offers me freedoms and choices*
versus *My dependence on my income has me stuck paying month-to-month for my over-
extended life.* If the former won the debate, you could easily take financial
risks or quit your job to pursue a different opportunity if you desired. If
the latter won, then you'd focus your efforts on minimizing your debt and
perhaps you'd stay at a job you didn't like for the sake of stability. These
are just two generic examples of the democratic brain process at work. At
any given time, there may be two or more conflicting truths presenting
themselves in our minds. The mind must decide in favor of one or the
other, and the winner of the debate becomes the reality we settle upon.

In order to decide upon a reality imbued with our own higher-order
values and creative thinking, we need our prefrontal cortex to be strong and
healthy. (That's the area of the brain behind the forehead which is respon-
sible for our ability to self-reflect, exercise executive decision making, and
have higher-order thought processes.) When the prefrontal cortex is not in
perfect working condition, we easily default to a reality derived from our
older, more energy-efficient fear responses. This democratic system enables
us to create plausible outcomes based on our experiences, but by no means
are these accurate accountings of what's really going on. In fact, David
Eagleman notes that the subconscious mind makes up ninety-five percent
of our brain activity. By the time we consciously think of something, it has
long been mulled over, debated, and processed in our mind for seconds,
minutes, hours, days, months, or even years. After spending so much energy
on these subtle processes, our conscious participation in the debate is as
simple as deciding if the glass is either half full or half empty—yet it is
actually *both* at the same time. If neither perspective is wrong, then neither
is completely right, either. So if our truths are not an accurate snapshot of
what's going on, then they just represent our *preferred* stories—and in some
cases, they might be outright lies.

Are you having trouble believing me?

WHO IS IN THE MIRROR?

Just think of the extreme example of body dysmorphic disorder (BDD), a mental state in which an individual sees a different image in the mirror than what the rest of us see when looking at the person. There is a heightened sense of concern regarding a physical attribute or perceived deficit. Although others do not recognize or acknowledge any disfigurement, those suffering from the disorder can truly feel disfigured. An anorexic may literally see an overweight person in the mirror, despite bones protruding through a gaunt frame. And a chronic gym fanatic might see a thin, scrawny figure, despite bulging muscles and an intimidating physique. The phrase "beauty is in the eye of the beholder" truly sums it up. Each of us is the beholder capable of finding the beauty or dis-ease in life.

Our brains plot, craft, construct, and orchestrate at a conspiracy level all the time. As part of this beautiful design, we have multiple areas of our brains involved in overlapping functions. This helps us retain functionality in the case of injury. Take, for example, memory. Declarative memory—the kind of memory we mostly think of—involves our ability to remember things we've done, places we've been, and other such basic information. It gives us the ability to declare we know something. This type of memory is generally associated with the hippocampus. Non-declarative memory is generally associated with the basal ganglia. This is the kind of memory you don't literally need to recall, but use often for procedural tasks, like remembering how to roller skate. Because we have overlapping functions in different areas of our brains, we may retain certain aspects of the function we call memory in the case of an injury. We store parts and pieces of these memories, like squirrels hiding nuts for the winter. When we are hungry for recollection, we unearth the parts and pieces and reassemble them for what looks to be a complete and accurate recall. Each time we remember an event or moment in time it is actually a reconstruction of pieces glued together with some help from logical filler or segues.

Unbeknownst to our conscious mind, the two sides of our brain are in an agreement to create a reality that works for us as individuals. Separately, the two brains skew us into imbalance; but thanks to the corpus callosum—the lengthwise center division in the brain—the two halves communicate and cooperate, fabricating a truth we decide we can live with. Each time we engage in this reconstruction, or memory retrieval, we fill in gaps of information with a storyline to create a seamless image. Without democratic cooperation between multiple areas of our brains, recalling our identities and histories might literally be impossible. It is much more complicated than this when you take into consideration the functions of the prefrontal cortex, frontal cortex, motor cortex, somatosensory cortex, parietal lobe, occipital lobe, and temporal lobe. So for the sake of narrative simplicity, I'll just talk about left versus right.

Putting Your Underwear on . . . Last?

The right brain is primarily concerned with experiencing the world *in relation* to other things. It has no capacity for time sequencing. It is a location hardwired for living in the **now**. Each thought is all that exists. There's no cause and effect, no rationale to explain things in a neat logical package—just full experience of the thought or moment. If you were to live only in the right brain, like some stroke survivors or individuals with brain injuries, you'd likely not be able to read, understand numbers, create a story line of your life, project what might happen if you engaged in a destructive action, show up to work on time, stay on task, choose the right words, and much more. You'd put your underwear on after your pants no matter how many times you were told otherwise. Additionally, the right brain defaults to spontaneity as its frame of reference, creating an experience of reality that feels in-the-moment and unified. To our right brains, we humans are all pieces and parts that make up a cosmic soup of existence. Do you remember those moments when you looked up at the stars in the night sky, completely overwhelmed and in awe of the unfathomable concept of infinity? That was your right brain taking control. Empathy, compassion, life's wonderment and awe are all possible when portions of the right brain are neurologically engaged. The phrase, "we are all one" is the right brain's basic neurological mantra. Dr.

Jill Bolte Taylor, a Harvard-trained neuroscientist and stroke survivor, gives a wonderfully succinct description of the right brain's abilities in her book, *My Stroke of Insight*:

> By its design, our right mind is spontaneous, carefree, and imaginative. It allows our artistic juices to flow free without inhibition or judgment. The present moment is a time when everything and everyone are connected together as one. As a result, our right mind perceives each of us as equal members of the human family. It identifies our similarities and recognizes our relationship with this marvelous planet, which sustains our life. It perceives the big picture, how everything is related, and how we all join together to make up the whole. Our ability to be empathic, to walk in the shoes of another and feel their feelings, is a product of our right frontal cortex. (pp. 30–31)

What Exactly Do You Mean by That?

To balance all of this, the left brain is primarily concerned with making logical sense out of our experiences. It busies itself with creating time lines of logical progression, mapping an event to a cause and its effect, and labeling our thoughts and moments as either past, present, or future. It uses those labels as comparison points for all other actions. It serves as our inner detective, deducing our personal histories. The left brain masterfully details, organizes, files, categorizes, and examines. It strives to create clearly delineated boundaries for thoughts, objects, and moments in time. It keeps us on track, on time, organized, analytical, ponderous, predictive, and problem-solving. The left brain is why we excel academically, why we understand that abstract shapes can be letters in an alphabet that makes words, why we speak a language that conforms to rules, and why we perceive *I* am *me*, separate from *you*. The left brain sets up behavior protocols and patterns—and the left brain quickly defaults to them as a response to new situations. One might say that the left brain values literal definitions, while the right brain values intuitive insight. If you were to live only in your left brain, then you'd experience the world literally— unable to understand sarcasm, puns, implications, relational patterns, interpret facial expressions, or differentiate an angry body gesture from a loving one. Dr. Taylor describes the left brain functioning in this way:

. . . [O]ur left mind thrives on details, details, and more details about those details. Our left hemisphere language centers use words to describe, define, categorize, and communicate about everything. They break the big picture perception of the present moment into manageable and comparable bits of data that they can talk about. Our left hemisphere looks at a flower and names the different parts making up the whole—the petal, stem, stamen, and pollen. It dissects the image of a rainbow into the language of red, orange, yellow, green, blue, indigo, and violet. It describes our body as arms, legs, a torso, and every anatomical, physiological, and biochemical detail one can imagine. It thrives on weaving facts and details into a story. It excels in academics, and by doing so, it manifests a sense of authority over the details it masters. . . . One of the jobs of our left hemisphere language centers is to define our self by saying "I am." (p. 31)

You may identify more with one side of the brain or the other, but ultimately our highest level of functionality depends on a healthy relationship between both sides. Our right brain communicates experiences to the left side, which then takes over and fills in the gaps of those experiences with a plausible storyline to tie them into a semblance of reality. Many of our self-told identity stories can be reduced by science to the neurological circuitry running through the brain. Even our clearest memories are not reliable accounts of the truth. Take, for instance, the common occurrence of contradictory eyewitness accounts of a crime scene. Was the assailant wearing a blue shirt or a red one? Did he have a beard or was he clean shaven? Was it a cell phone in her hand or a gun? Three different witnesses will give three different descriptions of the same person. What are the factors that influence individuals at the same place, at the same time, to see completely different realities? Why is it that during an argument, one person hears one thing while another hears something else? The answer is that there's a sub-story generated by the brain, which then creates what the person believes he is experiencing. While it sounds fantastical, the truth is that the inner world often creates the outer experience—not the other way around. So it's in our best interest to have that inner landscape—our right and left brains—in cooperation rather than conflict. Instead of getting into an esoteric debate over the nature of reality, I will illustrate it by describing this intriguing exercise.

IF IT WERE A SNAKE, IT WOULD HAVE BITTEN YOU . . . BUT WHAT WOULD A GORILLA DO?

There's a great video I have been showing for years in my workshops with law enforcement agents that emphasizes this point well. It works with anyone, actually, but it has a profound impact on law enforcement audiences because their level of awareness on the job is one of their strongest and most important survival skills. It's simply called "An Awareness Test." The beginning of the video starts with a voice instructing the viewer to count how many times the basketball team in white shirts passes the ball. The video then shows two teams playing a game: white shirts against black shirts. During the middle of the game a man in a gorilla suit walks out into the center of the court, bangs his chest nine times, then walks away. At the end of the video the audience is asked to recall how many times the team in white passed the ball. At this point everyone eagerly answers, proud of their level of awareness. Most do well, but the answers do vary a little. However, when asked how many saw a gorilla, it's usually less than fifty percent. In the groups of people with whom I've facilitated this exercise, it's more like fifteen percent at best, with a good portion of the audience looking dumbfounded and confused. I usually hear, "What gorilla?"

How can a group of individuals have selective blindness to something directly in front of them?

The answer is because our brains fabricate the truth of what we sense based on what we have either *already* experienced or what we *expect* to experience. Our capacity for attention is limited to one thing at a time. (There are those of us who pride ourselves on being multitaskers, but the truth is that we just do multiple things with less efficiency and skill because we are actually busy quickly switching our limited attention back and forth.) This is exactly why a room full of officers who *expect* to be questioned about the amount of passes will only see the ball passes. Their field of vision (controlled by the occipital lobe) processes what is *seen* using some of these sub-stories. The expectation set at the beginning of the exercise acted as the sub-story that told them what to perceive.

Consider this exercise I recently did with a law enforcement agency. Immediately after showing them the video I lied and said I was now showing them a different, yet similar video in which something completely unexpected was going to happen. About 90% of the audience noticed the gorilla. They were primed to see it with an expectation. They were shocked when I told them it was the same video. If we spend most of our internal energy on setting up references to our past experiences or preparing for our expected experiences, then our attention is mostly in the past or the future. Holding items in our attention requires lots of brain energy. So when we spend most of that energy attending to things that are not really in the present moment, we leave very little to recognize the here-and-now. How much of *now* do you miss by being in the past or the future? How many silent sub-stories do you tell yourself, just under the surface, which literally alter the images you see and the reality you perceive? It's probably impossible for you to know.

Our brains fill in these story details all the time. Although this gets us into trouble over and over again, it is also the essence of our amazing human potential. Recently, my daughter and I were drawing a picture. She followed directions very well, and her picture was progressing beautifully. I clearly noticed she was frustrated. She had a lump in her throat and her drawing took on some sabotage qualities where she purposefully over-erased or drew extra hard to rip through the paper. Finally, she said multiple times that she wasn't very good at it and she couldn't do it. I told her that was just her story, and that I believed she was a good artist and getting better all the time. She looked at me and said, "but isn't *that* just a story too?" Out of the mouths of babes! I agreed—yes, it was just a story. Then I said, "But which story makes you feel better, causes you to work harder, and helps you problem-solve when you want to give up?" If the brain makes up stories, and we claim those stories to be truth, then why not consciously create new stories—equally plausible—to rewrite our truths? It is our choice.

We see this narrative principle used in cancer treatment centers where patients visualize their own cellular healing: their white blood cells as victorious armies attacking pathogens and shrinking tumors. These methods are used because they show results. The placebo effect is now scientifically proven to be as effective an intervention as drugs in pain and depression studies. Isn't this a case of the thinker crafting and creating a new persuasive story to shift the body into a new reality? If these new positive visuals and stories heal the mind and body, then what do you think the old negative ones actually do to your health?

I promise you, you are *not* going to like the answer.

Exercise 2: Which Brain Do I Rely on More

The purpose of this exercise is to become familiar with which side of your brain you lean on more. No side is better than the other. Write down your preferred choice for each of the five questions in your dedicated journal.

Note which statements feel most comfortable to you.

1. A) I really value being organized.
    B) I feel taking time to organize wastes time I could be using to experience something else.

2. A) I feel that planning helps me make the best use of my time.
    B) I feel limited and restricted when I plan out my time.

3. A) I think structure and rules help communicate clear and useful boundaries.
    B) I think structure and rules limit my potential.

4. A) I value science and fact-based information as a way to make sense of my world.
    B) I value inspirational experience and intuitive knowledge as a way to make sense of my world.

5. A) We have to fend for ourselves in this world.
    B) We have to help each other in order to survive.

Remember, we use both sides all the time. This exercise simply gets you familiar with the side you tend to lean on more. The more familiar you are with your brain's comfort zones, the better you will be able to create two-way communication in the later exercises. If most of your answers were choice **A**, then you tend to lean on the left-brain functioning. If most of your answers were choice **B**, then you tend to lean on the right-brain functioning. Note in your journal which side of the brain you prefer to default toward.

Chapter 3

YOUR STORY, YOUR HEALTH

"The world as we have created it is a process of our thinking. It can not be changed without changing our thinking."

~ Albert Einstein

By now you've pondered the concept that our minds fabricate our reality or at least embellish on it enough to cause each of us to experience the world differently from one another. You've contemplated the intricacies of perception and the power of our self-told stories. While the brain seems to run the show, where would our minds be if not for our bodies which contain them? The mind-body relationship is complex and intimate. Not only is our world perception a process of our thinking, our body health is, too. Here's the tricky part: Not all of the thinking that informs our bodies happens at a conscious level. Remember, conscious thought makes up the smallest portion of the brain's functioning. It's hard to believe that our entire understanding of who we are actually uses the smallest amount of brain matter and energy. What is going on with all the rest of that space?

BE CAREFUL WHAT YOU THINK; YOUR BODY IS LISTENING

In the last chapter, we talked about sub-stories that dictate what our memory stamps as real and what our eyes are able to see—or *not* see, as in the case of the gorilla. The very same sub-stories running just below our consciousness speak volumes to our bodies in each moment. And if you think your body isn't hearing them, you're absolutely wrong. Take a brief moment to remember the worst nightmare you've ever had, the one that jolted you out of bed with a wave of fear—heart racing, skin damp, lump in the throat, breathing shallow, emotions charged. Why did you react that way? It was just a dream—not even conscious thought, right? You reacted that way because you were functioning from your limbic brain.

I'll take a moment to pause here so we can recognize that you might not be interested in brain science the way I am, but you can still benefit from knowing a bit about how your mind works behind the scenes. I have been meditating most of my life, oblivious to these brain mechanisms. My meditation practice was just fine, and I felt like I was lacking nothing. However, learning about the physiological side of things deepened my practice, facilitated even more healing of my own trauma, and connected dots I didn't even know needed connecting. So I will keep it high-level and relevant in the hope I can shed some light on some of your own patterns and behaviors which today are shrouded in mystery. What you're about to read is crucial to illuminate the way you deal with your stress, regardless of its nature.

THE PRIMITIVE BRAIN

The limbic brain is basically considered a primitive brain concerned with basic survival mechanisms such as fear, flight, food, and fornication. In your dream state the amygdala—an almond-shaped area of the limbic brain which is active during dreaming and the fight-or-flight response— creates a story line that sets off a variety of neurological messages to your body. "Reality" has no influence over your body's response; otherwise, as in the case of your nightmare, you would have remained calmly sleeping in bed with deep and even breaths and a resting heart rate. Instead, as you dreamed of the monster chasing you, the amygdala shouted "DANGER!" Like a willing subject your body not only listened, it actually responded. The amygdala doesn't know the difference between past, present, and future. So whatever happens in your dream is interpreted as happening *right now*, in present time, to your body.

So why is this dream process important to your stress?

The answer is because the amygdala engages far more often during our day-to-day than is healthy. It takes the smallest perceived threat or stress sent to it by any number of its many inputs and initiates reaction in the body just like in your dream. Many of those negative stories we tell ourselves, like the ones in Chapter One, keep us in a low-level state of danger or fear response. We become oriented toward the world from a place of negative associations. Since we have more neural pathways devoted to recognizing threat than to recognizing positive stories, this pattern is very easy for us to fall into. Remember my old story about not being tall enough? That story engaged in many situations in my life, just below the surface. Because I mapped new encounters to that old one, my fear response turned on slightly at seemingly benign moments. For instance, meeting a new friend of the same sex who was taller often engaged that sub-story so that I'd soon have to spend lots of energy trying not to feel threatened or territorial or to compare myself to her. Once I got into the comparison because I felt threatened, the game was over as the story of "I'm not tall enough" won out. At that point my self-esteem plummeted. I'd experience stomach upset, tension in my jaw, repetitive negative thoughts, inability to focus on anything else, and sometimes mild nausea during extreme cases.

At each instance of this type of threat response, hormones, neurotransmitters, and body processes chip away at one's ability to remain healthy and balanced. In simple terms, here's what's going on: A thought or situation occurs and the senses send that experience to the temporal lobe where the hippocampus determines if it's threatening. It does this by referencing this new experience against situations in storage that share certain similarities. In my case, I'd reference a tall female against a negative association of being short—one I developed as a small child. If the hippocampus decides that a tall female is threatening, the experience engages the amygdala—more specifically, the HPA-axis—where the pituitary gland and adrenals become involved by producing adrenaline and cortisol. These hormones normally prepare our bodies for either fight or flight (or even freezing), like running from a predator or battling an assailant. They increase blood flow to muscles to increase our reactivity time and short-term strength. They increase our peripheral vision and heighten our senses. They metabolize glucose for quick energy. They keep us functioning like a well-oiled machine in the face of imminent danger. The problem arises when the story doesn't actually come from *real* imminent danger. As in my case, the threat came from my perception. In cases like this there's nothing to literally react to, yet our bodies ready themselves and flood with hormones anyway. This is the situation for most of us. Our hormones engage, often with no real outlet. If there's no real threat then what do we do with all those powerful hormones and our readiness response?

WHERE'S YOUR "ON" BUTTON?

Here's a simple exercise I do in my workshops that will give you firsthand experience of this. Wherever you are right now, take a two-minute break. Close your eyes and think of the most immediate stress in your life. Perhaps this is financial, spousal, professional, or involving health or family. Think about the situation, the emotions involved, the people involved, and the level of unfairness. Allow yourself to feel the emotions associated with this event. Once you've got that experience clearly in mind, note each of these areas of your body to gauge what's happening.

- Your forehead—are you tensing between the brows?
- Your jaw—are you clenching?
- Your throat—is it dry or have you stopped swallowing?
- Your neck and shoulders—are they tight or drawn up?
- Your chest—is your breathing shallow or constricted?
- Your heart—is it beating faster?
- Your gut—does it feel queasy or like there's a pit inside?
- Your knuckles—are your hands relaxed or tensed?
- Your lower back—is it tight and contracted?
- Your thoughts—did they turn to hateful words or negative self-talk?
- Any other part of your body you'd like to notice.

If you noticed a response or condition in any of the areas listed (likely more than one) then you can easily see the result of your amygdala turning on your adrenaline and cortisol, because this is exactly what you just did. Think about this: You did that to your body with *one* thought. How many times a day does a worrisome thought flit across your mind's eye? If you are like the rest of us, you do this to your body every day, probably multiple times a day. Now, go shake off all of that or think of something funny before you try to concentrate and read further.

Man versus Animal

If you're an animal in the wild and you've managed to fight your way out of imminent danger or were lucky enough to outrun your predator, you would find yourself a thick bush to hide under. Here, you'd shake and twitch involuntarily as the adrenaline and cortisol dissipated out of your body. Once your nervous system regained equilibrium you'd go about your life with very little to no stress damage. Dr. Peter Levine notes in his book *Waking the Tiger* that studies indicate something about animals in the wild—they don't typically suffer stress-related diseases like Post Traumatic Stress Disorder (PTSD). But we are not animals in the wild. To maintain our illusion of civilized behavior, we pressure ourselves to remain functional, calm, level-headed, productive, all with little regard to the storm raging inside our bodies. Due to our belief that we are separate from the animal kingdom we seem to ignore the fact that our stress response functions in exactly the same way as an animal's does. We're supposed to be above all of that, right? Biology says an intense adrenaline rush can take hours of deep sleep to completely dissipate. Depending on your life's circumstances or your chosen profession you may experience these adrenaline rushes daily. This is the case with the law enforcement personnel I work with. Their level of stress exposure far exceeds what "normal" society experiences. Regardless of your profession, whether it's the narrow avoidance of a car accident, the sound of a siren close by, the image of a tragic crime, the scare of financial ruin, or the fear of not being able to meet a deadline, we rarely have the opportunity to drop out of life to sleep it off for ten to eighteen hours. Can you imagine telling your boss or family each time you were stressed that you'd be unavailable for normal day-to-day functioning for up to eighteen hours in order to find balance? I know that wouldn't work in my world.

Maybe Getting Right Back in the Game Isn't Such a Good Idea

We are a culture that prides itself on picking ourselves up by our boot-straps, dusting ourselves off, and jumping right back into the game. And nowhere in this process has anyone thought to tell the adrenaline and cortisol it's safe to turn off. The less time or attention we give to "coming down" off our adrenaline rush the more we store it up, increasing our sensitivity to this hormone. I use the metaphor of torque stored in our muscles, cells, and tissues. Imagine a static picture of two cars at a standstill. In the picture both drivers look the same. The sensory information you receive as an outside observer shows you two identical cars, two identical drivers, therefore two identical situations. However, what you don't know from the outward appearance of the picture is that one car has the engine turned off and the other one is on. The driver in the second car has the gas pedal to the floor and one foot on the brake. Which car will fishtail, swerve, and need extra help regaining control when the starting gun fires? So if the un-dissipated adrenaline is stored up, increasing our readiness to action just like the car, what happens when we're full and that one incident puts us over the edge? Have you ever experienced the argument in which you explode and years' worth of stuff comes out like a spewing volcano? Control, clarity, and navigation at that point are extremely difficult.

Additionally, as these neurotransmitters and hormones continue flooding our bodies over time we develop a predisposition to Type II diabetes, cardiac arrest, stroke, fibromyalgia, addiction, obesity, neurological disorders, autoimmune disease, asthma, Parkinson's disease, Alzheimer's, depression, PTSD, and sometimes suicide—just to name a few. We mentioned the hippocampus as the part of the brain that decides if something is a threat that needs to be routed to the amygdala. Sadly, it's also the area of the brain involved with signaling the "everything's okay" message and turning down the very response it initiated. Dr. David Perlmutter and Alberto Villoldo note in *Power Up Your Brain: The Neuroscience of Enlightenment* that sustained stress actually causes free-radical damage directly to the hippocampus. Think about it—the mechanism that turns on the stress response is also key in turning it off, yet it suffers damage by the very process it regulates. So the prognosis is that we get stuck in stress cycles based on our stories and we damage ourselves enough to lock us into imbalance, depression, and disease, flailing in the dark for a shutoff valve we've destroyed. I know this from firsthand experience, reliving old trauma as though it were always fresh. I experienced the accidents that caused my temporary blindness many times over, had hyper-vigilant and out-of-context reactions to flying objects like Frisbees or softballs, and broken out in cold sweats and panic if something got in my eye. It took years to break these loops of deeply grooved trauma. Soon, you'll be looking at some of your own experiences that keep you stuck in this cycle.

THE RECORD STUCK IN THE GROOVE

If we know sustained stress is so bad for us, then why don't most of us give time and attention to letting off some of this steam?

One reason might be that society views the symptoms of this healing process in a negative light. Think about what it felt like for you after your most intense fear or scare experience in your life. Common symptoms of dissipating adrenaline can include shaking, shivering, total exhaustion, the mind wanting to zone out and go blank, little desire to socially interact, and compromised ability to cognitively be sharp or have in-depth conversation. Because these symptoms tend to make us less productive and less social, we think of them negatively and often avoid them or become embarrassed by them. But we're actually avoiding the very process our bodies require to bring us back to equilibrium. Remember, we pick ourselves up, dust ourselves off, and avoid the natural process of healing. In fact, within the law-enforcement industry, there's a need to spike the adrenaline over and over to help avoid the symptoms of the come-down. Frequently officers find themselves retelling, reliving, or listening to their friends' traumatic stories because they get a spike of adrenaline which puts off the dissipation just a little longer.

With no preventative attention, this cycle has the potential to run amok and turn each of us into mini time bombs, just waiting for the adrenaline rush that puts us over the edge. Humans cannot sustain indefinite amounts of these hormones. You can't fill a tank more than full; it ends up overflowing. It is no coincidence that officers in this country suffer a greater risk of suicide just after retirement than most people. Actually, their risk of suicide is much higher than most throughout their entire career, but it increases even more after retirement. They've filled up with the highest levels of adrenaline they can sustain and without an outlet and no support system they crash and burn precisely when they are supposed to be enjoying the retirement they've earned.

In a nutshell, the brain is a master storyteller, weaving fact and fantasy into every moment. The limbic brain believes all of the stories and is particularly good at activating the traumatic ones. It then uses them as a justification to spur its armies into action, even when new situations only *slightly* resemble the old traumatic ones. The techniques printed in Part II of this book that address this cycle are not always readily available to the masses. They are taught in alternative institutes, often concentrated in cities with a metaphysical demographic. I've only ever found two other books that document them for general consumption. It is my firm belief that the general population need not struggle to find help, nor have to live in a certain demographic area to get the assistance they need. One should not have to swallow foreign or challenging dogma to begin a personal healing process. The exercises that appear later have done wonders for my clients and my own ability to calm down my limbic brain, dissipate the adrenaline, and erase the active charge of the traumatic events that have peppered my life. Once I understood the physiology, my trauma became my guide, my informant, and a doorway to my own healing.

So there is good news—great news actually. *You* are the master magician who can make the elephant in the middle of the room disappear!

Exercise 3: Body-Mind Connection
The purpose of this exercise is to become acquainted with your body's reactions during certain mental states.

Directions
Part 1: Sit in a comfortable place, alone and uninterrupted. Remove any pets as they may cause distractions. Begin by breathing comfortably for a minute or two at your own pace. Concentrate on the way the breath feels going into your nose, down your throat, and back out again.

After a few minutes of breathing refer to your **I AM** list. Do this exercise for each item in the **Aspects of Myself I Easily Accept** column. Allow your mind to say the first phrase of the column. I am. . . . Take a minute to notice any body sensations, tingles, or twitches as you repeat this. Try to notice what areas of your body your awareness goes to as you say each item from this column. You can start at your toes and work your way up, or start at your head and work your way down to systematically notice all parts of your body.

Note your feedback for each item on the list in your dedicated journal.

Part 2: Repeat all of part one, including the breathing preparation, but this time do it for each item listed in your **Aspects of Myself I Do Not Easily Accept** column. Notice where you store or manifest beliefs associated with those aspects of yourself that cause you conflict or resistance.

Congratulations—you are becoming aware of how your body and beliefs communicate when you are quiet and attentive enough to notice.

*"The true value of a
human being is determined
primarily by the measure
and the sense in which he
has attained liberation
from the self."*

~ Albert Einstein

Chapter 4

MIND MAGIC—INTENTIONAL REWIRING

SCIENCE . . . EVOLVING WITH THE BRAIN

Up until the early half of the last century, science and the medical field supported the idea that once a part of the brain was damaged, the abilities it controlled were lost forever. They thought you could not regenerate anything lost or damaged. As we continue to evolve as beings, fortunately, our science does, too. It has since been proven that the brain has vast abilities to regenerate, reallocate, and rewire. Abilities lost to brain damage or stroke can be revived and can even migrate to other control areas. The ability of the brain to change functionally and structurally is called neuroplasticity. The magical part is that our own *experience* acts as the catalyst for the brain's ability to change. To add mystery to magic, consider this: Science has discovered that the *experience* need not be anything more than a perception, story, or belief. When the prefrontal cortex *perceives* an event—or even *perceives* it's in control based on the story we're telling it—those stories begin to sculpt our mindscape. The stories one creates subconsciously and consciously actually create a physical reaction in the brain. When we imbue those stories with details and emotional content, they become marked in our brains by dedicated neural pathways and networks.

The more we tell these stories, the more embedded the networks become as they repeatedly engage. It's like digging a groove slowly over time, and before you know it your wheels are locked into a deep groove directing your path. The deeper those grooves are, the less effort it takes to engage that pathway and the more energy-efficient that particular reaction becomes.

In recent years, science has been able to track brain functioning in those who meditate and practice mindfulness. The results show that meditation engages precisely the areas of the brain involved in controlling and minimizing our stress levels. Additionally, those who meditate seem to grow new neural pathways, release "feel good" neurotransmitters, increase their capacity to learn, increase production of beneficial growth hormones, and actually repair certain areas of brain damage (as in the hippocampus).

Not only does the brain rewire itself, it also births new brain cells well into old age—an idea once thought preposterous. This ability is called neurogenesis. The bottom line is that the brain is *not* set in stone. We are not dealt an unchangeable hand. Individuals who solve puzzles and crosswords, are involved in problem-solving, and keep their mind active by planning, working with numbers, meditating and learning new things can retain their cognitive ability well into old age. In fact, evidence shows that individuals can recover cognitive ability in just the same way. But just how much control do we have over this amazing phenomenon of neuroplasticity? Maybe Lake Placid offers some insight.

HOCKEY, ANYONE?

In 1980, Lake Placid, New York, hosted the winter Olympic games. The hockey games that year would go down in history as "The Miracle on Ice." The competing Soviet team had an impeccable record and was considered the greatest hockey team in the world. That year Herb Brooks, the American coach, was determined to take his team of amateurs and college players all the way to a victory at the Olympics. In a matter of six months of rigorous training, he did what no one believed possible: He led the American team to Olympic victory over the favored Soviets. Herb Brooks employed intense mental training, as his philosophy was that the fastest skater is only as fast as his mind. He combined aggressive mental exercises, positive thinking, and visualizations with rigorous focus. This guerilla-style mental training was at the forefront of his regimen and because of it he went on to work a miracle. His mental training philosophy is commonly used in sports training today. In various experiments with control groups brain scans consistently show that mental training grows new neural pathways—connections in the brain that carry information regarding the visualized activity. Performing the action and visualizing the action in detail activate the same pathways in the brain. It's just like creating a new file folder on your desktop and filling it with topic-specific information. Since the mid-'80s, sports psychology has been considered a viable subcategory of psychology and has adopted the practice of performance-enhancement visualizations as a main component of professional athletic training.

THE MIND'S EYE

Let's back up. If the body reacts during a nightmare from an image in the mind's eye, it's clear that the *visual* is the director of the body's response. Now we find out that the mind's eye has the ability to change the brain mapping by creating new pathways that transmit new information. Are you beginning to realize the vast implications of the images you create for yourself? The stories you tell yourself, whether consciously or unconsciously, actively chart pathways through your brain. Think of it this way: If, as a child, you experienced something traumatic—such as I did when my right eye got sliced by a flying object—you would then have developed a negative association with many of the event's factors. The amygdala takes snapshots of the moment and makes emotional associations with images in the snapshot. In my case, I developed a traumatic association with small flying objects and an obsession with eyes. My limbic brain stored and encoded the picture of the flying object as dangerous and threatening. After the accident, every time I experienced close proximity to a small flying object, my hippocampus related that to the similar circumstances of my accident, set my amygdala to threat mode, and caused my entire body to panic. Each traumatic reaction engaged the original traumatic neural pathway, deepening the trauma groove over time—fortifying that reaction and causing me to relive that experience. Like a train hooked and led by a track, my obsession with eyes caused me to think of the accident often, activating that same neural groove with just the thought. When the limbic brain pushes the body into fear it diminishes blood flow to the prefrontal cortex. The prefrontal cortex, to be brief, is capable of emotions such as empathy, compassion, and joy, and is also involved with functions such as goal setting, motivation, and problem-solving. So if our blood flow to this area diminishes when we feel fear, fear then keeps us out of the prefrontal cortex and virtually incapable of experiencing joy, finding creative solutions, or even learning anything new.

This cycle is detrimental and downright vicious. The more we're in fear due to our experiences of the past or an expectation of the future, the more we reinforce negative neural pathways and stifle our own ability to find a way back to joy. It's a no-win situation. This is why PTSD is such a brutal disease. The sufferer literally can't find her own way out of a repeating traumatic event. It could even be argued, but never proven, that my intense fear and obsession with my eyes attracted my adult accident in which I burned both eyes with hydrochloric acid. I'll talk more about that later on.

Dr. David Perlmutter, neuroscientist, and Alberto Villoldo, Ph.D., note that

> *Neural networks are created by focused, engaged stimulation . . . the choices you make actually do influence the physical structures, the neural networks, in your brain. 'Experience coupled with attention leads to physical changes in the structure and future functioning of the nervous system. This leaves us with a clear physiological fact . . . moment by moment we choose and sculpt how our ever-changing minds will work.' On the other hand, when we don't pay complete attention to what we are doing in the present moment, our brain activates a host of other synaptic networks that can distract*

it from its original intention. So, attention matters, whether it is gentle meditation or the intense concentration of an athlete at a critical competitive moment. (pp. 72–73)

They go on to say that

Being involved in stimulating mental activities—such as problem solving, exploring novel environments, and, perhaps most important, meditating regularly—enhances BDNF (Brain Derived Neurotrophic Factor) production and creates a brain that is not only more resistant to deterioration but one that enables you to push the limits of day-to-day functionality. In this context, it is important to view meditation not as a passive activity but as an active, brain-stimulating exercise. (p. 92)

So with focused attention we can rewire our neural pathways. That's a nice theory model, but discovering and teaching *how* to put that into practice has been my mission. I am motivated by interesting theory, but I thrive on application. One of the things always frustrating to me during my lifelong meditation practice has been vague directions or implications that I should just embody certain states. Statements like *be in the moment* always left me more confused than I was before, as that statement rarely came with a how-to guide. There are a few exceptions to theoretical models that made a profound impact on my meditation practice. My studies with the Ishaya monks offered me a much-needed process through which I learned some concrete tools to help me cope with the stress of my life. Subsequently, the techniques I document in this book—some of them derived from the curriculum of the Berkeley Psychic Institute which I studied at a sister-school in Denver—represent a few of the most concrete tools I learned or created. These tools have found a daily place in my life and my clients' lives.

How it All Works

Here's a little bit of preparation for how this all works. I will use the example of a technique the trauma world calls **Name It and Tame It**. It's a technique in which traumatized individuals or those in crisis are taught to reframe their words. Instead of saying, "I *am* angry," or "I *am* afraid" the individual rephrases to "I *feel* angry," or "I *feel* afraid." This rephrasing precipitates an immediate (and measurable) reduction in blood flow to the amygdala. Conversely, when one uses *I am* statements there seems to be a direct association with the emotion and the individual continues to feel that emotion, remaining stuck in that experience. Substituting *I feel* statements seems to put the individual in an observational mode, describing the emotion. When one instantaneously observes and then labels an experience, the blood flow increases in the prefrontal cortex and decreases in the amygdala, thus calming down the fear response center. This particular exercise is a favorite with my private law-enforcement clients.

Let's take this idea one step further. As we know, when the prefrontal cortex hears stories that make it believe it's in control, it has the power to regulate the limbic brain fear response. The more the prefrontal cortex can pay attention to the story and engage in the principles of neuroplasticity—experience plus focused attention—the more the prefrontal cortex can quiet the limbic brain. So visualizing detailed and vivid stories seems to speak the language the limbic brain understands. If those stories are detailed in a positive way, then the amygdala receives a message that this new information is non-threatening. The hippocampus begins storing positive stories as a reference point. With enough repetition and attention, the next time the hippocampus tries to reference a situation against a need to engage the amygdala, it will find positive associations, and it will reroute the situation to the neocortex for logic processing instead of the fight-or-flight response.

In plain language, this is how it works: In healing from my eye trauma, I told myself new stories around my vision, my eyes, my vulnerability, and my sight—over and over again—until, eventually, I stored enough positive stories in my brain. I created new neural pathways with "eye" associations and information, and I overrode the traumatic fear response for the majority of my eye triggers.

My experience has been that the exercises presented in Part II will calm down the fight-or-flight response as the first step. They lay a foundation and offer a language with which to examine some existing stories in a neutral environment, and they begin the process of crafting new ones.

Mindfulness exercises have been shown to activate an alpha brainwave pattern, creating a ripe environment for relaxation and intuitive insight. They offer the prefrontal cortex increased blood flow, neural stimulation, and neurotransmitter flow. They increase the thickness of the cortex through consistent engagement. The brain experiences new learning with each use, and it reinforces neural pathways, enabling the prefrontal cortex to override the amygdala during unnecessary engagement. Neurosculpting® has been my mind's fitness program. In my Neurosculpting® workshops, individuals report amazing amounts of insight, release, and emotional access after just the first exercise.

What's in it For You?

You do not have to be traumatized to see the benefits of this in your own life. Are you telling yourself stories of lack that keep your mind preoccupied so you never recognize opportunities of abundance? Again, remember the gorilla and selective blindness. Do you tell yourself stories of poor health and keep your body in disease? Perhaps you tell yourself stories of poor self-worth, so you never see when others believe in you. Are you surrounding yourself in your professional life with horrific crimes so that you never see the good in people? Maybe you tell yourself stories that you need to win over others to survive, so that you cannot soften your own boundaries. Do you believe the world is a place of distrust so you are never able to be vulnerable with anyone? Have you defined success as something that only happens to others so that you are unable to move ahead in your career? Whether your stress level is mild or severe, the physiological process is the same. Because all I have to share with you is *my* own experience, I'll invite you into how my life trauma informed me about my own profound healing abilities at various points in my life. For some, these next few chapters may seem extreme, while others may wish their trauma was so slight. I am not sharing this with you to compare trauma levels or evoke pity but to show you that viable information and healing can come from any trauma—actual or perceived.

Exercise 4: Do You Agree with Your Brain?

The purpose of this exercise is to see if your cognitive (conscious) identity associations match your brain's subconscious identity associations.

Directions

Part 1: On a clean sheet of paper, make four columns. Title the first column **Aspects of Myself I Am Most Proud Of**. Skip the second column. Title the third column **Aspects of Myself I Am Least Proud Of**.

Look over your two lists from Exercise I. Using your own judgment decide which are the top two attributes from the list **Aspects of Myself I Easily Accept** that you are most proud of. Note these items in the first column. Repeat this process for the **Aspects of Myself I Do Not Easily Accept**, but instead of the top two items you are most proud of, decide on the top two items you are least proud of. Note these two items in the third column.

Aspects of Myself I Am Most Proud of		Aspects of Myself I Am Least Proud of	
Responsibility		Self-absorbed	
Attentive mother		Impatient	

Part 2: Label the second column of this exercise **Aspects of Myself My Body-Mind is Most Proud Of**. Label the fourth column **Aspects of Myself My Body-Mind is Least Proud Of**.

Sit in a comfortable place, alone and uninterrupted. Remove any pets as well as they may cause distractions. Begin by breathing comfortably for a minute or two at your own pace. Concentrate on the way the breath feels going into your nose, down your throat, and back out again. After a few minutes of breathing, refer to each of your items in your **Aspects of Myself I Easily Accept** list from Exercise I. As you think about each one, note the level of intensity each one causes in your body. Some may cause no body reaction, while others may create twitches, stomach activity, tingling, rapid thought generation, or various other experiences. Note the two items that caused the strongest reaction and write them in column two. Note the body reaction next to the attribute.

Repeat this process for the **Aspects of Myself I Do Not Easily Accept.** Observe the two items that cause the strongest reaction and note them in column four.

Aspects of myself I am most proud of	Aspects of myself my body-mind is most proud of	Aspects of myself I am most least proud of	Aspects of myself my body-mind is least proud of
Responsibility	Responsibility (head tingled)	Self-absorbed	Unfocused (began to salivate)
Attentive mother	Playful (stomach gurgled)	Impatient	Impatient (breath quickened)

Compare the first and second columns, and then the third and fourth columns. Note if your mental preferences match your Body-Mind preferences. If they are in sync, then congratulations—your conscious mind is aligned with your subconscious ideas on this topic. If the two sets of columns differ, then congratulations—you've now noticed that your conscious mind is on a different page from your subconscious ideas regarding this topic. You may have some powerful sub-stories that live just beneath your conscious detection.

"Few are those who see with their own eyes and feel with their own hearts."

~ Albert Einstein

Chapter 5

BLIND... TWICE: HOW TRAUMA INFORMS HEALING

Earlier, I mentioned my issues with my eyes. I will give you an account of both accidents and the resulting mental states I found myself swimming in for years. These accidents framed a perspective I carried between the ages of eleven and twenty-one. This perspective shaped my fears, reactions, behaviors, and obsessions during some very formative developmental years. There's an old saying that it's not the destination but the journey . . . and it is the same with trauma: It's not the event itself, but one's *perception* of the event, that creates the trauma. This became evident to me only after my second accident.

BLINDSIDED

The first time I remember encountering real serious physical trauma was when I was eleven—just before I started meditating. It was a random accident, yet there was a split-second moment of awareness that happened just before the incident which caused me to know what was going to happen—a premonition of sorts.

My older brother and I were playing together in my room. He was my playmate in the truest sense of the word—fun, caring, attentive, creative, and quite hysterical. In the early '80s, it was popular for girls to wear their hair in big sweeping waves fastened with clips that looked like mini combs with long teeth. I had a collection of those clips; my favorite ones were metal with sharp edges on the top and sharp teeth in the comb. The sharp ones were the only ones that dug into my heavy curls and held them in place all day. They were shiny and looked like gold. The size, shape, and luster of these clips are burned into my memory. This particular day my brother and I laughed as he propelled small toys up into the air like mini helicopters. He placed the toys in the center of a leather belt he held slack in his hands, then snapped it taut and hard. The toys catapulted up to the ceiling like out-of-control puppets. We thought this was hysterical.

He reached for the comb.

He hadn't even snapped the belt yet, but I remember everything went into slow motion. I have yet to understand the slow-motion effect, but it happened exactly the same way with the later eye accident as well. I screamed hysterically before he snapped the belt, and to my recollection, I ran into the corner of the room. I hid my head and yelled, while trying to protect my eyes. I was deathly afraid he'd spin that comb right into my eyes. What prompted that thought? Had I seen that on television? Heard something like that in a graphic story? I had never experienced anything like that before, yet the fear was quite specific. Whether this is an example of what some call premonition or just an example of an overly cautious and imaginative girl, my protective actions preceded the actual event.

Then he snapped the belt.

Instead of flying up to the ceiling like all the other toys had done, the comb spun across the room like a Chinese star and sliced into my right eye. The rest of what I remember of that night is almost as if I were a third-person observer. I felt my body, but my recollection in my retrieved memory is as though I observed the event.

I fell to my knees screaming, crawling into the hallway with my eyes covered, as my parents frantically ran upstairs. There was nothing my mother could do to get close to my face. All I wanted was to keep my hands over my eyes and be in darkness. I saw my mother from some other vantage point in the room. She carried me into the bathroom. I remember her persuasively talking to me, trying to get me to open my eye. It was too bright, and I was too scared. By then it was late in the evening, and my parents didn't know the severity of the injury . . . how could they, I wouldn't let them see. As children are likely to be dramatic, my mother eventually talked me down until sheer exhaustion took over.

I fell asleep. By this time I hadn't opened either eye for a few hours. My mother sat by my bedside—holding my hands, keeping me from touching my eye in my sleep. My memories of this moment are not of being in the bed, but of watching from the corner of the room as my mother sat vigil. I remember also noticing my body in bed, but only from the neck down.

EYES WIDE OPEN

The next morning it wasn't until walking down the hallway toward the ophthalmologist's office that I opened my eye for the first time since early evening the day before. Everything was sharp with painful clarity and the tears just kept coming.

I remember every detail of that eye exam—the smell of the waiting room, the children's *Highlights* activity books on the table, the strange head restraint, the angelic blue examination light I've come to associate with healing, the doctor's face so close to mine I thought his nose would touch my nose, and the shutter that clicked past my field of vision like a windshield wiper as he magnified his lens to get a better look. Unfortunately, we didn't get the first prognosis from him—it actually came from another mother in the waiting room . . . in the worst possible way you could hear such news.

After my exam, the doctor asked me to wait in the waiting room. During that time, another patient—a young boy—went in to see him. A little while later, the boy and his mother returned. She clearly didn't realize we had seen the doctor already. When my mother asked her, out of polite and conversational concern, "How is your little boy?" the relieved woman answered, "He's going to be okay, according to the doctor—much luckier than the little girl that was just in there before him!" I remember going numb at that point as I thought, "*I* am that little girl!" As a mother now, I cannot fathom what my own mother must have felt. My heart sinks just thinking about the few times my own daughter has been under the weather. Each of us at that moment added another layer to our traumatic experience—fearful anticipation of the unknown. It was strange to watch another woman's relief come at my own expense. (I'd later learn in my brain studies that a fearful experience of uncertainty does large amounts of stress damage to the brain.)

The doctor finally told us I'd need to go directly into surgery, no stopping home for personal items and no short detours. My right cornea had been sliced dangerously close to my pupil. Upon hearing this news, my attention must have shifted to a completely different internal story as there seem to be gaps in memory. I don't remember the ride to the hospital or the surgery room itself. Yet I have vivid recollection of the anesthesia mask and counting backwards from 100 to 98. After the surgery to stitch my cornea back together, I remember being hazy and begging for water out in the recovery room. For years I felt the way the word "Nurse!" garbled out of my dry and burning throat. I got ice cubes instead of water. It was frightening that night to fall asleep, alone, in a strange place without my family. The hospital smell is very specific, its antiseptic quality delivering wafts of isolation and sterility. I missed the smell of my own room, sauce cooking on the stove, and even my parents' cigarettes which I hated so much. I was allowed to have visitors the next day and the whole family came. I remember how sheepish and apologetic my brother was. Even though I was the one who was hurt, I felt intense sadness for him as I thought about the guilt he might carry.

A MASK OF BRAVERY

The operation had been successful and the level of vision damage would reveal itself over time. After a few days I returned home. I distinctly remember walking into my house, hanging up my jacket in the closet, and proceeding to the kitchen to pour a glass of orange juice. My mother seemed very proud that I was self-sufficient so quickly. I actually felt like a drone, noticing how each and every normal act felt somehow different with one eye. I received a huge welcome back to school and lots of accolades for being so brave. I didn't think I was brave. I felt shocked and at the total mercy of the doctor and luck. I felt as though life had thrown me into a spinning washing machine and I came out disoriented. Sometimes we can mistake silence for bravery.

I spent the next few weeks with my eye patched as the stitches remained. Fear only grew as I got closer to the day I'd have the stitches removed. They were not the dissolving kind of stitches. I was asleep for the actual eye surgery but had to be awake for the two different stitch removals. They only removed half the stitches at a time, with a week or more in between, to make sure the tear was healing. I was made to stare into that amazing blue light in a completely dark room as the doctor emphasized that I was not allowed to blink. I felt a slight tugging and pressure on my eyeball as he moved tiny blades around the stitches in my cornea. I held back vomit and the urge to blink. I drenched myself in sweat and held my breath. I prayed a lot. I remember not wanting to blink for a week because each time I did I felt one of the knots of thread scraping against the inside of my eyelid. I had the unique pleasure of having to wear a funny pink plastic dome-like patch with holes in it for a few weeks. At eleven and in the fifth grade, I was now interested in boys. My healing seemed to just add insult to injury; I looked like a fly. I took school pictures late that year. They put me in a side- profile pose to get my good side.

THE GIRL WITH CURIOUS EYES

But soon my vision completely healed; my scar was only noticeable to me when I looked at my iris in a magnified mirror. Life seemed to carry on just as before. It wasn't long, though, before my traumatic experience found its own expression. I began to notice strong knee-jerk reactions and intense fear around sports with flying objects. I'd panic completely at the gesture of slingshotting a rubber band, paper clip, or rock. My "friends" thought it was funny. I remember one of my friends at the time put a tennis ball in a tube sock, held one end, and flung it at my face like a weighted bungee. She laughed as I panicked. Kids can simultaneously be so premeditated yet unaware.

In my early teens, I began to cut out the eyes from beautiful models in magazines and store them in a jewelry box. I grew my collection and would from time to time marvel at all of these attentive and staring brightly colored paper eyes, which had no ability to blink. I'd rustle my fingers through the collection, having no idea that it might relate at all to my previous experience. In my young adulthood I wrote and published a horror story in *Deathrealm* magazine called "The Girl with Curious Eyes." It was about a girl with the very same paper eye collection who had body dysmorphic disorder. She ended up cutting her own eyes out. Amazingly oblivious to my own expression of traumatic symptoms, it wasn't until a friend asked if the story was autobiographical that I then put the pieces together.

From seconds *before* the incident, my brain devoted story-telling time to the narrative of my trauma—adding frightening experience to the incident, over and over, until my behaviors and compulsions began to manifest. The story became so powerful it overwhelmed my body and I began to write what I thought was fiction. I was simply continuing the old narrative by finally putting it on paper. By then I had been meditating for a long time, but I was still years away from understanding how to selectively apply my meditation practice to my mind's stories.

After all those years of subconscious focus on the story that eyes are vulnerable, painful, dangerous, and expendable, is it any wonder I ended up right back where I started—recovering a second time from a horrific eye accident? Only this time, my healing felt intentional and different. I was ready to rewrite my story.

THE STING OF IRONY

Now I was nineteen and in college studying to be an engineer, although I never became one. Organic chemistry was my least-favorite class, but the lab was interesting. On the day of my accident the lab was about to get much more interesting . . . for everyone. We were conducting a super titration experiment. That meant the chemicals involved were much stronger than normal, so we'd have to use them under the glass hood—the fumes alone were enough to hurt you. Here's an amazing irony—during the years since my first accident, I had been hyper-vigilant about eye protection. So the fact that this was the *one* day I hadn't put my protective goggles on first was totally astounding. The teacher gave us our instructions and left the room briefly. I collected up my bottles of chemicals and lined them up in front of me. The bases and acids were all there. I picked up the glass jar of super-concentrated hydrochloric acid, which—to my great dismay—was slippery. It slid right out of my hand, crashed onto the high table, and again life switched into slow-motion.

Every drop of acid mobilized in a torrent of tiny daggers aimed directly at my face—each approaching with strobe-light motion. Drops burned up my nose, the bulk of the acid assaulting my eyes. This must have been my movie-influenced memory here, but I recall hearing the sizzling *sssss* as the acid seared into my eyeballs. (I don't actually know if acid makes that sound when hitting eyes at all.) I took a deep breath, froze in that amazingly powerful limbic "play dead" option, and declared with staccato words and not enough air, "HOLY SHIT!" The acid drops were the last visual image I had for the better part of a week.

I was paralyzed, totally unable to help myself—the only thing running through my mind was the mantra, "I am blind." My lab partner froze as did everyone in my close proximity. I heard commotion as Chuck, a classmate, jumped over the desks from across the room and grabbed me with his large hands. I don't remember anyone else's name from my chemistry class, not even the teacher's—but Chuck's name is there forever. He ran me over to the wash station and we both tried to pry my eyes open— the pain was too great and the water spray too harsh. I couldn't breathe. It was right then that the teacher returned to the room, no doubt thrown in to a horrible scene of both his and my negligence. I am fairly certain that a few times during that week, he feared for my health, his job, and his long-term career. I am not the litigious type, and I was always clear that the accident was my fault.

In the emergency room, they swabbed some sort of cream into my eyes. When the doctor asked me the concentration of the acid, I answered, "Six molar." He responded, "Did you mean .6?" I reiterated my answer. Remember, this was a super titration, so the concentration of the acid was way beyond the concentration of our regular lab experiments. The doctor whispered under his breath, "Oh shit." This is *nothing* you ever want to hear your doctor say as he's tending to your emergency situation. Again came the mantra, "I am blind." He told me he had no prognosis for me at all. He couldn't assess the damage to my eyes, nor could he tell me if I'd ever be able to see again. What he did tell me was that I burnt most of the nerve endings in both eyes, and that they would likely hemorrhage for a long time. I was alone, in the ER, with a dismal and completely shattered reality.

And this is how they sent me home.

"Heal" is no Longer a Four-Letter Word

I slept in my bed at night and each morning my parents moved me into their room to lay there for the better part of the day with the TV on. My eyes were sealed shut—swollen. It was about four days before I opened them. But this recovery felt very different from my first accident. The moment the acid hit my eyes, I became convinced—rather resolved—to the new reality that I was blind. I pushed myself into problem-solving mode immediately. The moment I got home, I called my boyfriend, who was away at school, and told him I may never see his face again. I searched for ways to process the grief and to hold on to images I had of everyone and everything. For four days in my parents' bed, I played movie after movie of my life's images, trying to note each detail and catalog it into my memory. I frequently thought about how to move around the house, how to sense my surroundings, and what I would now have to do to become functional again. I remember feeling gratitude for the years of sight I felt I had borrowed from age eleven until then. I didn't for a minute stop to wallow in limitation. I thought about ways to finish school, what my day-to-day would be like trying to get dressed, move around, and learn how to become self-sufficient. I was devastated and swimming around in a surreal fishbowl of confusion, but not once did I spend energy on victim mentality. I simply thought, "Damn it, girl! You got yourself into this stupid mess, now you have to figure a way out." I attribute this gift of toughness to growing up in New York and the fact that by then my prefrontal cortex was much more mature than when I was eleven. Finally, I could strategize and problem-solve.

My prove-it attitude carried me through that first week as I was determined to become independent, no matter what the state of my vision. Without knowing exactly how it happened, I rewrote a victim story to one of determinism, independence, and even heroism. At the end of the first week, I opened my eyes to a painful display of intense bright light and dark shadows. Clarity would come much later. Light was painful to my burnt nerves. Over a short period of time, I regained enough shadow/light vision to move around. Eventually, that turned to a hazy blur—possibly what those who are legally blind see without their glasses. I was still extremely light-sensitive and had to wear dark sunglasses during the day and inside. I returned to school after two weeks to sit quietly in the front, wearing dark glasses—barely able to see the board. One eye healed faster than the other. As my light sensitivity diminished, I was able to wear an eye patch over just the more damaged eye. Here I was, eight years later, wearing an eye patch . . . *again*. By now I realized my vision was worlds better than I had ever hoped it would be, so I was happy, relieved, and in total gratitude for my healing and my vision. One eye hemorrhaged for a few weeks, but the patch hid that well. I had no white in one of my eyes and by then it had become a party trick to lift the patch and let people see glowing red eyes. Some thought my pirate patch was a fashion statement. I actually remember a guy at a party telling me how sexy it was.

HINDSIGHT IS 20/20

My eyes and sinuses recovered completely; I again had 20/20 vision, no scars on the outside, and some interesting shifts on the inside. I credit my astounding healing to my problem-solving attitude and my complete gratitude for each small stride—and, of course, Chuck and my family. During that recovery time, I convinced myself I was capable of anything. This is the story I burned into my brain each time I tried to relive the drama. Traumatic revival converted to gratitude and triumph. Over and over, I began to repattern the traumatic memory of this accident. It's totally amazing to me, even though I lived it; the process of simply writing about the first accident in this chapter caused me to stop writing multiple times and use some of my own techniques in order to calm down and continue with this chapter. My heart raced, I broke out in sweat, and my limbs shook. Yet recounting the second accident, which was actually much worse, brought out pride, gratitude, and joy. I remembered each accident with radically different body responses. This was a huge clue that my specific mental states during and just after each accident wired my brain differently to my trauma experience. Remember, trauma does not come from the event; it comes from our *perception* of the event. Since I instantly reframed my victim mentality to one of heroism in the second accident, I have no mental or physical traumatic reactions to that memory.

Trauma informs us that we have stories, still active, directing our responses to something that is no longer present. Our aversions, body signals, panic, and fear all point to something stored inside that wants to speak out. Instead of reliving trauma and retelling our story, we can rewrite it. Many trauma survivors get an adrenaline rush recounting their stories. This rush reinforces that traumatic experience. But we can choose to tell new stories—even regarding old events. We can paint ourselves as the master, the hero, or the problem-solver, so that each time we retell the old story, it brings up emotional responses which don't engage the limbic brain. We can choose to tell stories that actually complete the action of the event differently, like those books in which you have options to choose your own endings.

My second eye accident became a rite of passage that showed me I was capable of anything as long as I continued to stay in problem-solving mode. I did not know then—but I know now—that problem-solving is a function of the prefrontal cortex. So as long as I told myself stories of my ability to adapt and looked for solutions, I kept the blood flowing to the prefrontal cortex and out of my limbic brain—the area that wants to keep me in my traumatic fear response. In fact, the prefrontal cortex doesn't really fully develop until our early adulthood. It may very well have been neurologically impossible for me to deal with my first accident in the same way I dealt with my second. My new stories literally sculpted my brain and gave me different cortical navigation capabilities.

The eye theme continued well into adulthood. In my early years of teaching I met the most amazing man who then became a dear friend. He is completely blind, has been since he was a toddler, and is a completely independent, intelligent, and charismatic high-school social studies teacher in a public school. He helped solidify my appreciation for sight, put the severity of my accidents into a new perspective, and reminded me of heroism every day.

But these stories were just one layer of stress; there was yet another layer to my limbic brain functioning that took me twenty-five years of trauma to understand. And this particular trauma, unlike with my eyes, was literally life-and-death.

Note: This is the last journal exercise before the meditations in Part II.

Exercise 5: You are the Victor
The purpose of this exercise is to practice rewriting a belief or memory to effect an ending of triumph rather than defeat.

Directions
Sit in a comfortable place, alone and uninterrupted. Remove any pets as they may cause distractions. Begin by breathing comfortably for a minute or two at your own pace. Concentrate on the way the breath feels going into your nose, down your throat, and back out again.

After a few minutes of breathing, envision an old memory in which you were wronged, hurt, defeated, humiliated, or embarrassed. Recreate the scene in your mind's eye just as you remember it, but pause at the critical moment just before the negative outcome.

Choose some of the **I AM** statements you are most proud of. Imagine using some of these qualities to envision a different ending to this story, one that puts you in a position to feel mastery, joy, fairness, pride, gratitude, or any other positive emotion. As you change that story ending observe any shift in thoughts, emotions, or body sensations. Imagine placing that new story back into the file you pulled it from—even if you have no idea where this is. Just pretend.

Note any feedback, thoughts or insights on a separate page of your dedicated journal.

Chapter 6

HIT BY LIGHTNING, CHARGED BY DEATH

"Strange is our situation here upon this earth. Each of us comes for a short visit, not knowing why, yet sometimes seeming to a divine purpose."

~ Albert Einstein

Up to this point I've talked a lot about our self-told stories and how they drive our behaviors. As I deepened my practice, I was better able to handle stress, my stories, and my own psychology. But there was a physical piece still eluding me which I finally put into the equation in 2009, when my lights practically went out for good. I must backtrack here to give the appropriate context—because it is vital to understanding how mental states work in conjunction with physical well-being. So let me go back to my fifteenth birthday.

A DARK CLOUD

It was July—my birthday, in fact—and I was turning fifteen! I spent a long weekend with my best friend at her family's summer house in the Poconos. We had lots of friends there, as we spent many summer weekends vacationing over the years—in her boat, hiking around, or on trikes, trail-riding through the woods. We enjoyed quite a lot of innocent freedom for young teens. On this particular day, about eight of us rode quads in the warm summer sunshine. What could have been better than to spend my birthday roaming free with friends on powerful motorbikes? But this perfect birthday was about to change my life . . . forever. A sudden storm blew in, and within minutes it got cold, dark, and began to pelt hail—large and freezing cold. This was strange for July and eerily ominous. Thunder boomed just overhead. We scrambled for cover as fast as we could. We jumped off our gear, ran for the closest house on the hill, and all huddled under the porch at the garden-level garage. A friend and I were leaning against the garage door, the long metal door handle spanning the distance across my lower back to his. It's always funny to see the false bravado of young teens—each of us feigning bravery against this dark and powerful storm. Suddenly, there was another crash of thunder and a flash of lightning . . . *my* lightning.

It struck somewhere along the side of the house, and like two rag dolls, we were catapulted off the garage, flying through the air with no control. We landed a few feet from the garage, face-first in the dirt. I looked up at my best friend, standing over me, confused. She stared at the two of us on the ground, her face aghast. The intense pain in my spine caused me to believe the boy had hit me hard, directly in the lower back with a sledge hammer. I asked him what he did to me. Puzzled and lying on the ground alongside me, he asked the same thing. That's when we realized the lightning came out through the metal garage handle, right through both of us. My back was in severe pain, but I was mobile, as was he: My wrist watch frozen in time at precisely that transformational moment. I wish I would have saved that as a memento, but I truly had no sense at that time of how profoundly that moment would shape my life. The friends got us home quickly. We came barreling into the house, wet and cold, the friends saying, "Lisa and Robby were hit by lightning!" I have a vivid memory of taking my wet socks off slowly, thinking, "Wet socks aren't a good idea when there's lightning." But as kids are known to tell tall tales and since both of us seemed just fine, none of the adults seemed fazed by the story. Out came the birthday cake. I have no recollection of what I wished for. I still felt all the pain, but I, too, doubted what had happened, simply because I was still alive and seemingly fine as I enjoyed my cake. But I wasn't fine at all and I wouldn't know it for a while.

That was the summer I started blacking out.

Exit Stage Left

My first episode—or what I call "exiting"—was shortly after the lightning strike, again in the same friend's house in Pennsylvania. I had these seemingly random moments of fainting spells. The first time it happened I was on my way to the bathroom as the world started to feel funny. I was tingly, my breathing was shallow, and voices trailed off into a distant place. I made it all the way into the bathroom, but not gracefully. I ended up knocking down the door with my limp body, crashing into the bathroom where my startled friend screamed. I awoke to my friend's concerned family. I slept it off and was fine the next day.

Over the years, these types of fainting spells occurred intermittently, and they were chalked up to hormonal changes. People around me at the time postulated many causes: dehydration, menstruation, getting up too fast, or having low blood sugar. My parents, who had heard about these episodes but witnessed very few, took me to the doctor who, after one blood test, said I was fine. I got absolutely no diagnosis. As time went by the severity of the blackouts worsened—and mostly when I was alone. I recall waking up on the bathroom floor on many occasions—the last conscious thing I'd hear myself say was, "Oh no!" Then the lights would go out and I'd exit. By this time the episodes were accompanied by intense confusion as I'd wake up in puddles, increasingly unable to regain any muscle control. I spent years wondering if I urinated myself during the blackouts, as the puddles were large but strangely seemed to cover my entire body-print on the floor. Sometimes I'd have to crawl back to bed and lay there for hours. Nobody witnessed as the blackouts continued. Whether or not I downplayed it, I can't remember, but it seemed to go unattended. I developed a fantastic practice in denial, and I treated each blackout as if it were an isolated incident—inconvenient but unremarkable.

Simultaneously for years following the lightning strike, my lower back was excessively sensitive to touch. A small area just at the lower lumbar region would send shooting knife-pain up my back, along both sides of the spine at a mere finger's brush. This diminished over the years until one day I realized it was gone entirely.

EXIT STAGE RIGHT

Fifteen years later, by the time I was in my early thirties, the blackouts were much more intense. The onset elicited great fear, as I knew the world was about to fade away. Recovery became harder and harder, to the point where I'd need an entire day and night's bed rest to regain strength. It took all of my waning energy and concentration simply to crawl slowly to my room. Speech was difficult and exhausting. On numerous occasions I awoke with bruises, black eyes, and once, jammed awkwardly halfway underneath the claw-foot tub stuck between it and the toilet. Sometimes during recovery I couldn't even rally to the toilet, content to allow nature to take its course right where I was. Movement incited the imminent need to vomit, so I'd try to remain still as buzzing and vibrating pins and needles coursed throughout my whole body. You know the pain of a limb that's asleep as it begins to get blood flow—those pins and needles screamed their way in and out of my limbs, with no way to shake them off. In those moments of slowly creeping consciousness, I found myself caught in an amazingly loud buzzing cloud. I remembered the Carlos Castanada books I'd read and wondered if I was meeting the deity Mescalito. It felt just like he'd described in *The Teachings of Don Juan*. What in the world was happening? I totally denied that any of the countless blackouts were related to each other. I never once considered I had something wrong with me or that any of this was out of the norm for most people. I thought, "Nope, this is just what happens to people."

I KNOW WHAT'S ON THE OTHER SIDE . . . AND IT'S ELVIS!

Finally, during a routine doctor's exam in my early thirties—seventeen years after my first episode, I told the doctor I felt faint. The next thing I remember I was rudely interrupted by a voice telling me to breathe. In my experiences, each time I'd pass out my consciousness seemed to continue. Although I knew something was wrong, I truly believed I was conscious and involved in some other activity—at least until the buzzing started and I realized *Oh, I'm not conscious at all.* This time was the same. I was involved in some video—acting, performing. And since I'm divulging my soul with this chapter I'll admit to you that I was in the video with Elvis. Truly: He was in his full white jumpsuit and we were preparing to perform a song. I was annoyed at the stranger who had come on set and interrupted the video shoot by yelling, "BREATHE!" I thought, "Don't you know I'm in a video with Elvis?" Then the buzzing started and all gears shifted into recognition that something *really* bad was happening. The video scene pixilated and disappeared.

I regained consciousness in the examining room to the doctor's ghostly white and panic-stricken face. He urged me to breathe while he held a needle of atropine above me. Atropine is commonly used for resuscitation and for spiking excessively low heart rates. What in the world was happening? Once again, the table was drenched, my clothes soaking wet, and I couldn't move. I barely had enough energy to push out whispers. That's when I learned I'd had a seizure and flatlined. He wanted to know why I didn't tell him I had this condition. As ignorant as this sounds, I thought, "What condition?" Seizures? No heartbeat? No pulse? No breathing? What could he possibly be talking about? I've never had a seizure in my life, or flatlined . . . um, except for *all those times* I was actually having seizures and flatlining! Could that have been what was happening to me for all those years?

VASOVAGAL SYNCOPY

That's when he diagnosed me as being extremely vasovagal. He said I had syncopy, which is just a fancy word for fainting. But in my case it was extreme—causing seizures and my heart and breathing to stop. Most people who are vasovagal have a few isolated incidents of fainting—I had been having intense episodes since I was fifteen. My vagus nerve signaled my brainstem to shut down awareness in all cortices at once—to stop central command and "play dead." In the evolutionary scheme of things, and in the animal kingdom, this response is a viable alternative to fight-or-flight and can sometimes save lives. When it's a response to trauma and perceived threat, it does no good for anyone. There is even recent medical speculation that this fear-paralytic response is a contributor to SIDS (Sudden Infant Death Syndrome or crib death). I can no longer count how many times I exited as the world disappeared. So, if my heart stops, I no longer breathe, and I turn blue and rigid, am I dead? If so, how many times have I technically died? And for how long each time? I know for sure that in the doctor's office I flatlined long enough for him to call the nurse and for her to go into the other room to get the emergency resuscitation kit and to ready the syringe with atropine.

There's very little to do about syncopy. The list is short—stay hydrated, don't get up too fast from a squatting position, and most of all, keep stress under control and deal with buried trauma. The vagus nerve does many things, some of which include keeping the body breathing and the heart beating. Damage to this nerve through disease, stress, trauma, or possibly even a lightning strike can cause a reaction like mine. At this point I still had no idea what kinds of stress or situations incited my episodes. The most recent two episodes in my life were the most traumatic and severe. These were the ones that caused me to understand this process more deeply and to eventually decide this will never happen again to me. My body couldn't take any more.

PASSING THE BATON IN THE TRAUMA RELAY RACE

In October 2007 I had a vasovagal seizure and blackout in front of my daughter, who was three at the time. We were in a grocery store having a bite to eat in the food court. I bit down hard into a chicken bone and to my recollection took her by the hand and went into the bathroom to examine my bleeding and loose tooth. I have detailed and complete vivid memory recall of how the tooth wiggled, the acrid taste of the blood in my mouth and throat, the image of her in my periphery as I stared at myself in the mirror, and my fear of losing the tooth. I remember hoping the dentist could save it.

*And this is how I **know** memory has little to do with accuracy, because that's not what happened at all.*

Remember, during these episodes my consciousness believes it's still the driver. What actually happened was that I bit into the chicken bone and blacked out instantly—knocking my head into my plate of food and falling over backwards onto the floor. I had a seizure, then flatlined and turned blue. Eventually, I heard that familiar buzz and the reality of the bathroom disappeared as I realized I was on the floor. I grasped at reality—*Wasn't I with my daughter somewhere? If I'm not in the bathroom then where am I? How long have I been here? Oh my god, where is she?*

Store personnel surrounded me. Paramedics were on the way and my daughter came running over. I could barely speak. She placed her hand on my chest and asked if I died. Might I say that absolutely *nothing* in my life prepared me for that moment. My heart sank as my daughter's illusion of safety was destroyed forever. I just wanted to hug her and tell her everything was fine. That's what a mommy does, right? She makes everything okay. I was devastated that my little girl had forever burned into her psyche the image of her mother having a seizure and turning blue. One incident, precipitated by a chain of events twenty-five years long, shifted my daughter into a reality neither one of us was ready for. A bit of her innocence was gone for good. We spent hours in the hospital, even though I didn't want to go, and I knew their tests would show nothing. Physical recovery from that one took about two days of bed rest—and I knew the episodes were getting worse.

It took a few weeks before my daughter stopped waiting on my every move, asking me if I was okay. This event began many conversations and exercises in dialing 911. We talked about death, illness, mortality, physical bodies, mental bodies, and any other huge and esoteric topic you can think of. Emotional recovery is still happening today.

THE FINAL CURTAIN CALL

The very next episode I had a year later, the last one I've had to date, was so severe that I decided it was going to be the last time I ever experienced this. Friends, my husband, and I were on my porch, talking. I had been angry at a social event the day before and unable to shake it—even though

I had meditated. I felt weird. I excused myself and went into the kitchen to get water. My husband felt something was wrong and followed shortly after me. He found me on the floor, rigid—my eyes wide open, my mouth a gaping maw. He told me it looked like I was frozen, staring at something frightening. He and a friend carried me onto a rug and he proceeded to shake me into breathing. Only this time I stopped breathing, over and over. It was so peaceful and still, and I heard my own voice say that it was so much easier to simply not breathe.

I had a sense my husband was with me, yet I felt completely peaceful in the long pauses of nothingness while I wasn't breathing. It was like floating in a perfectly still lake—effortless and serene. I never had this much trouble coming back, nor had I ever had this much enticement to stay on the other side. My husband continued to rock me each time I turned off, coaxing me to breathe. Interspersed in these moments was the image of my daughter and my family. I eventually began breathing with no more prompting. An hour or so later, he crawled with me up to the bedroom, where I remained for a day. I am so grateful for his wisdom and nature, and thankful my daughter slept through the event. I could not put her through that again. That was it—the last straw. I felt at that moment that if I ever had another episode then I'd never come back.

I needed to understand why this had been happening to me for most of my life. I knew from deep introspection and interoception that emotional events preceded my episodes, and in some cases I could identify specific content. But I needed to know more. That's when I learned the limbic brain has three choices, not two: fight, flight, or *play dead*. I learned that some animals can play dead so well that their nervous systems believe it and they actually die. Was this what I was doing? Each time my stress level got too intense or I encountered some subconscious trigger, was I choosing the *play dead* option? Was I so skilled at that natural coping mechanism that, over time, my body began to believe it? This was my theory—unproven by anyone. But I proved it to myself, just one year later.

Victory—Terrifying and Exquisite

I was encountering severe stress—meditating regularly, of course, but needing a physical release. I felt myself heading for an episode. With only seconds of warning time, I yelled, "NO!" I made the decision that I'd override my default option and choose to fight instead of play dead. I didn't have a blackout that day, but I did unleash such rage and terror in what seemed like a total meltdown—it was no wonder I'd never wanted to go that route before. Stuff from my childhood came up as ugly as I could have ever imagined. I heard myself ranting, screaming, and crying about unspeakable things. But I rode it out, didn't flatline, and had a victorious sense that I'd never have to have another episode again. And, once again, I have the deepest gratitude for my amazing husband; he witnessed it all and made it okay for me to brave my own storm. It couldn't have been easy.

I want to take a moment to recognize that I have a fantastic family and wonderful memories of childhood. I am perfectly clear that what came up for me the day I chose not to blackout may not have even been real, as the limbic brain believes any tale it's told. So for me, the accuracy of the mental imagery is irrelevant. What is extremely relevant is that I allowed emotional associations to finally bubble up, then dissipate, so they no longer lived inside me. My lifetime practice of mindfulness allowed me to recognize, participate in, and simultaneously observe this whole process. I felt as though I had witnessed a miracle.

It was at this moment that all the pieces clicked into place, making sense of my life's traumatic mysteries. I carried deep emotional trauma—it's no wonder I needed to start meditating at twelve! The lightning strike heightened my nervous system's sensitivity. When I couldn't rewrite my stories or even identify them, then the next option was to shut down my body. The link between my body, my life, and my stories was now crystal clear. My limbic brain had been running the show—rather poorly, at times. I learned that my meditation practice and stress-management techniques, in conjunction with limbic brain reprogramming and tremor shaking, could reshape the landscape of my brain and my behavior and transform my life. I became the navigator, mapping my own mindscape.

I am quite sure my wiring changed at the lightning strike, changed again after years of meditation, and yet again after I overrode my play-dead response. It is through these experiences that I've found a common language with those suffering traumatic stress. It is through my own trial and error that I found what really works to relieve and rewrite these patterns. As I've said before, I love a good theoretical model; but what I love more is having actual methods and tools to deal with what life throws at me.

And the plain truth was that my life wasn't going to be rewarding, graceful, or effortless until I cleaned up my big internal mess!

Chapter 7

PUT YOUR OXYGEN MASK ON FIRST

Up to now we've learned of the amazing benefits of interoception—awareness of our inner stories and thought patterns. If there are such benefits, then why don't we learn to do this as small children?

INWARD TO OUTWARD

We spend most of our lives focusing on the outside world. What clothes should I wear? What food should I buy? Where should I live? What school should I go to? What job should I get? Which mate should I choose? What car should I drive? What friends should I pick? What hobbies should I engage in? Where should I go on vacation? How should I get out of debt? How should I untangle this situation? How should I help others? How will I get help? And on and on. In most of our moments we place our attention outside of ourselves and do a dance with people, places, things, systems, institutions, and organizations.

Once upon a time in school, as tiny children, we were encouraged to go inward to our imagination and play pretend. It's what we did best at that age: play house, play cars, play monsters, play heroes, play school, sing songs, make crafts, draw, and tell stories. At some point it all shifts. Remember the daydreamer in your class in school who got in trouble for letting the mind drift to inward landscapes—maybe it was you. This was the case with one of my brothers.

When he was in the fifth grade, during his parent-teacher conference, my parents were told he was a daydreamer. His grades suffered and he struggled a bit in a traditional school setting. It wasn't until high school that he enrolled in the alternative program and excelled academically. Meanwhile, he's one of the smartest people I know!

We are asked to make a shift at some early point from inward to outward. This shift is born out of necessity. In order to function in the society we grow up in, we must make room and give attention to all of these outward demands. And so the daydreamers who are lucky enough to balance their dreams with practicality become functional and successful. Those of us who don't balance it well, but are lucky enough, become productive artists of some sort. Sadly, those of us who don't balance it at all become removed, sometimes isolated—often dysfunctional according to society's standards. In my experience, if I stayed inward or outward too long, I became a mess. Focusing on my outer world for too long left me reactionary, emotionally stunted, angry, judgmental, and often exclusively stuck in my limbic brain or left brain. I judged my own value by the success I had in my career, the number of friends I had, the amount of money in my retirement fund, or by my accumulation of material possessions. My concern for what others thought of me was stronger than my ability to act with integrity.

Focusing exclusively on my inner world left me a bit ungrounded, caught up in fabricated stories, missing the world around me, socially left-of-center, and a bit hazy. I could easily ignore problems by escaping to a place where they didn't exist. Instead of finding solutions, I found vacations—only to return to problems stubbornly waiting for me. This is simply my own experience with these two states. I am not implying your experience is the same. I am, however, encouraging a balance and a dialogue between the inner and outer landscapes.

To put it in as black-and-white terms as possible, I like to reference this excerpt from *Power Up Your Brain: The Neuroscience of Enlightenment*. Dr. David Perlmutter and Dr. Alberto Villoldo do an amazing job of making this type of content accessible and relevant.

Which Brain Are You Using?

Is your life a struggle for survival? Are you forever trying to make ends meet financially? Are you living hand to mouth? If so, then your reptilian brain is in the driver's seat of your cognitive apparatus.

Do you learn your lessons through difficult love relationships? Does your prince turn into a frog with a drinking problem after the honeymoon—just like your previous prince did? Are you always ending up with abusive bosses or business partners who never seem to appreciate your contributions? If so, then your emotional mammalian brain is predominantly in charge of your consciousness.

Does your intellect get in the way of your passion and joy? Are you forever analyzing things in your head? Do you fail to listen to your instinct and your intuition? Do you mistrust anything that is not proven scientifically? Are you disconnected from your feelings and insensitive to the feelings of others, even when you try not to be? If so, then you are trapped and bound to the fiendishly logical aspect of the neocortex.

Or are you flighty and ungrounded, with your head up in the clouds? Do you walk into a room and forget what you went there to do? Are you more conversant about quantum physics, the bloodline of Mary Magdalene, and international conspiracy theories than about your children's homework or what is happening in your neighborhood? If so, then your consciousness is probably in the grip of the prefrontal cortex.

If you are experiencing a predominance of any one of these brains, it is a sign that the parts of your brain are not acting in concert with each other, that those in the background at the moment are allowing another part to dominate and exhibit only its limited traits.

In actuality, to experience brain synergy it's necessary to be aware of your financial situation and your relationships; it's good to think officially and to dream with whimsy; and it's vital to keep all of these mental activities in balance with each other. (p. 27)

We're not going to get as detailed as above by compartmentalizing all the different brains. I will simply separate it into outer world and inner world. My experience, and that of my clients, indicates that if you attend to one and not the other, the imbalance eventually causes pain either emotionally, physically, mentally, spiritually, or logistically. The result is that we begin to believe we are ineffectual in creating our own realities. We easily buy in to the idea that we are victims or mere objects being pushed around by what life has to throw us.

We've all experienced ourselves saying things like, "If only my job weren't so . . . I'd be able to . . . " You can fill in the blanks. I have come to despise *If only* statements. They place responsibility and control on forces outside of ourselves, giving us permission to remain helpless, immobile, and victimized. Although it's sometimes true that we are powerless to change external factors, it is never true that we are powerless to shift our perception of those factors. Our brains neurologically respond mostly to our *perception* of the world, then behave accordingly. So if you're wondering why you can't become successful, shift your finances, heal your relationships, or gain confidence, I will ask you to think of the in-flight directions the stewardess gives when you fly.

Put Your Oxygen Mask on First

This is the approach I take with the exercises in this book. You cannot hope to effect great change in your outer world, your home life, your financial life, or with your career or relationships if you do not attend to your inner life as well. Remember the gorilla video—the inner story told the audience what to expect and, consequently, they could not see what was in front of them. If your inner story tells you that you are in lack, you can literally blind yourself to opportunities of abundance. Your stories don't have to be about high-level trauma in order to demand change. If you create stories of poor self-worth, invalidation, pain, and punishment, then how can you expect to have an outer world that's rich, abundant, fulfilling, and compassionate? You can not change or heal anything if you put a bandage on the outer wound and continue to scrape at it from the inside. It astounds me that the inner and outer worlds have been so segregated in our lives: Financial classes that focus only on money, school that focuses only on academics, music classes which only focus on theory, relationship classes that only focus on outer communication, and so on. You've heard of as above, so below; now I offer you a companion phrase: *outer mirrors inner.*

In my case, I needed to clean up my inner stories before my outer world stopped reflecting them. Once I cleaned up my story of being too short and needing to prove myself, my relationship to my friends and partners improved and became more relaxed. Once I cleared up the trauma story of my eye accidents, my ability to physically and mentally heal increased drastically. Once I discovered the layers of information available in my blackouts, I was empowered to stop the pattern and reach others in traumatic cycles. The world opens up in ways unexpected as we tend to our inner clean-up. The brain stores everything we've ever experienced, including connotations, associations, implications, and judgments. We have vast information inside ourselves waiting to inform our individual transformation. We wire ourselves through our experiences and perceptions. In essence, we get ourselves into this mess, so why is it so strange to believe we can get ourselves out?

Just as we create and turn on our adrenaline switch with limbic associations, so can we create the off button as well. Think about it: Meditation directly affects limbic brain activity, which keeps us in our negative stories. Regular meditation measurably decreases blood flow to the limbic brain and increases it in the prefrontal cortex. Those who meditate show different mapping on brain scans than those who don't meditate. Mindfulness practice reduces free-radical production and, specifically, damage to the hippocampus. These practices can positively impact one's cognitive abilities, decrease predisposal to dementia, increase immune strength, and much more.

I've spent most of my life searching for my on and off buttons, sometimes stumbling upon them after painful repetitive lessons, sometimes having bursts of revelation. I'm about to present you with the simplest and most direct ways to create that off switch, to rewrite that story, to rewire your brain, to clean up your inner landscape, to better your health—to map your mindscape and to transform your life. Don't let the apparent simplicity of the exercises fool you; each of these can cause deep transformation and rich personal discovery.

These exercises are a combination of my own and some I learned in the curriculum derived from the Berkeley Psychic Institute. Four of them came from my studies in that program, and two of them are exercises I created for myself and my clients. Although I have never been told I must not publicize them, I've seen very few individuals actually do it. I've always wondered why these techniques aren't in basic handbooks in every school, in every corporation, and in all realms of our society. My clients have been listening to my audio CDs for years, guiding them through these techniques. But now it's time for you to be able to access them any time you want, in the comfort of your own home, without draining your bank account to do so. In offering these to you, I am wishing for your transformation, healing, and your ability to effect great change in yourself and in others. Like waves in the ocean, each time you use these techniques, you create a ripple effect reaching far beyond your understanding.

Take a short break before reading Part II. Get a bite to eat, relax, have something to drink, go for a walk, or simply enjoy a moment outside of the pages of this book—because when you proceed with intention, everything will be different.

PART II
NAVIGATING
A NEW PATH

Chapter 8

HOW TO GET STARTED IN YOUR NEW PRACTICE

"The gift of fantasy has meant more to me than my talent or absorbing positive knowledge."

"Problems cannot be solved at the same level of awareness that created them."

~ Albert Einstein

I want to emphasize that when it comes to your own mind, *you* are your best authority. What I suggest in these next chapters are merely guidelines for you to begin your practice of stress management and inner awareness. You should trust what feels right to you and become increasingly comfortable with your own information. There might be methods I suggest that do not work for you in the same way they've worked for me.

These exercises are more than simply ways to address your stress: They are practices in discovering your own truth and information. We spend much of our lives focusing our attention on the outer world, so much so that we have to ask others to give us insight into ourselves. There's nothing wrong with a little help, but we need to also understand ourselves in order to navigate well. You are free to use these exercises in any order you like—independently or as a sequential set. You are embarking on a practice of mastery.

STRUCTURE

Each of the main exercises is structured in two ways. The first example of the exercise is more introductory and doesn't focus as heavily on discovery—although there is a level of discovery with each. The second example of each exercise takes the practice a little deeper and encourages different ways one can elicit more personal information. This version of the exercises calls upon some of the information you noted in your journal from chapters one through five. There are no right or wrong experiences, as the results are uniquely *your* experience.

Often my clients want to interpret the experiences to make sense of it all. I understand this impulse all too well. You are free to interpret your own experiences if you like, but know that a cognitive understanding of what happens isn't necessary at all. Your cognitive association with the world happens in another part of the brain, and that association has little to do with the positive impact the exercise has on your health and mindscape. It can be a challenge for some to have their cognitive analysis marginalized like this. So if you want to interpret, feel free, knowing that most, if not all, of the healing and benefits happened already in the experience of the exercise. What your conscious mind offers is an afterthought. Think of it this way: If you consciously interpret your dream after you wake up, it doesn't change any of what you *experienced* while you were dreaming.

For those who prefer a logic approach, here is a mechanistic breakdown of the physical process happening with each exercise:

1. Breathing to begin a parasympathetic response and slowing of the thoughts.

2. Activation of the prefrontal cortex to initiate synaptic activity and neurological mapping.

3. Deactivation of the amygdala to disengage old neuronal stress and fear patterns.

4. Deactivation of the stress hormones.

5. Orbito prefrontal cortex participation in creating a new story to direct, or sculpt, a fresh neuronal pathway to encode in the hippocampus.

6. Labeling of the new pathway for quick and easy access.

7.   Repeated usage of this pathway to override the amygdala response.

Obviously, this is a very generalized explanation, but it is a basic list of what happens whether or not your conscious mind is involved in the interpretation of your experience.

Spiritual Approach

Some of you may find your way into these exercises through a more spiritual approach, as I did initially—and that's just as viable. You can view these exercises as an open dialogue with your higher self as a way to align your beliefs, nature, psyche, and physiology with your ultimate path. I have found an inner peace, akin to the kind I've found in prayer, with these techniques. I have used this approach to cultivate compassion and empathy, which has caused me to view situations differently. I have been able to look at my vices and virtues, find and give forgiveness, explore unconditional love, and play with vast innate healing abilities. I have also used these techniques to delve into my darkest self, to open up a conversation with the most scared and ill-tempered parts of my spirit, and to bear witness during times in which my behavior was little more than reprehensible. You can ritualize these practices in any way that works for you, and you can fit them in to any existing spiritual practice you may already have.

In the Image Of. . .

As an important note you are also encouraged to change the imagery of each exercise a little each time to find what works best for you. Each exercise involves imagery created in your mind. There's a strong neurological reason to alter that imagery on a continual basis. As we create new stories, or perceive something new or different is happening, our prefrontal cortex activates because it's being told, "pay attention, something unfamiliar is going on." This process of *learning something new* fires up neural activity and we begin to release neurotransmitters like norepinephrine, dopamine, and acetylcholine. These neurotransmitters are essential in our ability to learn, focus, inhibit distraction, motivate to work towards goals, regulate our moods, problem-solve, make good choices, encode neural pathways and memory, and much more. These transmitters are essential in our ability to learn, focus, inhibit distraction, motivate to work towards goals, regulate our moods, problem-solve, make good choices, encode neural pathways and memory, and much more. The following exercises engage this area of the brain and these neurotransmitters. This practice creates a new neural map and stamps in the new information by sending electrical and chemical signals along this newly dedicated pathway (although the most recent research implies that sound may also be involved in the transmission of these signals).

Once the details of the visualization or meditation become rote or mechanical, it may no longer feel like you're learning something new or you may no longer need to pay attention. Information and processes that no longer require conscious attention—such as brushing your teeth or riding a bicycle—tend to migrate to the basal ganglia portion of the brain. You don't have to think about how to execute these activities each time; the process is automated.

The goal with this practice is to keep firing up the neural pathway associated with the specific new information so that it becomes an often-engaged and deeply embedded groove, just like the deeply embedded grooves we create by repeating our negative stories in the new context of current situations. Keeping up neural activity or the perception that something new is going on is as simple as changing one small visual from each exercise every time—like using a different color, shape, or texture. Novelty excites the brain in precisely the way we want in order to heal and transform our stories. This is why each exercise begins with an opposite folding of the hands. It becomes a non-threatening but unfamiliar sensation to alert your prefrontal cortex to wake up.

THE LOGISTICS

You can fit each exercise into a time frame that works for your busy life. I suggest taking about ten to fifteen minutes for each in the beginning, then tailoring them as you need. Early in my practice it was helpful for me to designate a regular time to do the exercises—like first thing in the morning or right before bed. I found that if I sat up, I'd have more experiences I could remember, versus lying down and falling asleep halfway through. I enjoyed a quiet space while doing these, but eventually I found I could use them anywhere, with my eyes open, as well. These changed for me over time. It's easy to trail off to some vague, unconscious space, or to fall asleep.

Don't get frustrated or think you did anything wrong—it may simply be what your body needs to do once you give it permission to relax. Enjoy those times and come back to the exercises over and over again. My guided audio CD, which covers the program outlined in this book, is available through the contact information at the end. If you feel you don't need guided assistance, simply read the exercises a few times before you do them so that the flow is in your mind—or you can have someone else read you the prompts as though they are guiding you. I had favorite exercises and resistance to others. You will, too.

Physiological responses may occur, and these may cause confusion if you are not prepared. It is common to have muscle spasms and twitches. During stress and trauma release, specifically the process of adrenaline normalization, one might experience twitching, spasms, and sometimes seizure-like tremors. Remember what animals do in the wild as their adrenaline levels regulate—they shake. You may, too. I have had many clients experience full muscle spasms and shaking limbs. I've even seen individuals flail on the ground with rapid shaking as though they were in seizure. *If* you know you are not ill or epileptic this can be very normal. My clients and I experience a great sense of relief just after the shakes pass. Other body sensations I've experienced include rapid onset of tearing, yawning, stomach activity, hot flashes, sweats, uncontrolled rocking, waves of emotion, and heightened olfactory or auditory activity. Many people don't experience any intense physical symptoms.

These are not just my favorite exercises. I'm presenting a complete regimen for you to use for the rest of your life. I've seen these techniques utterly transform individuals who felt they were on their last threads of sanity. Do not underestimate the opportunity you have in your hands simply because the exercises seem easy. Although you never need to go any deeper with any of this to experience a profound change in your relationship to stress and fear, this is also just the beginning of what's available. There is no end to the depths to which you can go or the number of techniques you can learn.

In Part III you will meet three individuals and learn their real stories and experiences with these techniques. I have spent thirty years accumulating techniques that work, not out of theory but out of necessity. I use all the techniques in this book regularly in my daily life and I have for years. During those times when I might "fall off the wagon," I am not a person I want to be around. It is in those moments that someone usually says something to me like, "You shouldn't be ungrounded. You teach this stuff." The truth is that I teach these techniques precisely *because* I am a user! There isn't a day that goes by that I don't get a validation or reminder that I need to meditate, find my center, and take a moment to heal.

YOU are your own solution. YOU have your own answers. YOU have the power to change your reality. YOU are the master of your own mindscape. You've already invested in this book, so let the exercises give you the greatest return on that investment.

Welcome to your new practice!

Chapter 9

GROUNDING

"Any intelligent fool can make things bigger and more complex. . . . It takes a touch of genius—and a lot of courage to move in the opposite direction."

~ Albert Einstein

I believe that simplicity is underrated. I first learned about the power of simplicity when I was at Tracker School lead by Tom Brown Jr., learning to live in the woods with none of our modern amenities. Time slowed down there. "To Do" lists disappeared and the needs of the moment superseded everything. Time and space boiled down to needs and resources in the most direct and simple way: If it didn't serve my direct survival needs, it was a waste of time and energy. This type of direct simplicity filled me with a sense of purpose, reverence, and resilience. Each small victory, whether it be carving my bow-drill, making a fire, brewing pine-needle tea, making a trap, or digging a water-still, had a direct correlation to my ability to thrive. This type of simple equation left me centered, grounded, and able to overcome discomfort and inconvenience.

Everyone has his or her own definition of feeling grounded or centered. It might be the feeling that life is flowing effortlessly, or when you feel perfectly comfortable in your own skin. Maybe it's when your purpose is clear. For me, being grounded and centered equates to those times when I'm less reactionary, more patient, clear about my boundaries without needing to take a stance, unshaken by competition or comparison, and present to more of what's in my environment. You will have your own experience of what being grounded and centered is like. For the sake of this exercise I will propose that being grounded means that *you are present, with full awareness of your being in its surroundings, without the distraction of the past or the future.*

I teach this technique to most of my private clients, all of my law-enforcement and first-responder groups, and at many of my Neurosculpting® workshops. This exercise alone is enough to transform an individual's relationship to stress and negative stories. It centers around two profound effects.

The first result of this exercise is a parasympathetic response for the nervous system. This response is associated with vasoconstriction, salivary flow, intestinal activity, blood diversion back to vital organs and away from muscles, and diminished blood-flow and neural activity in the amygdala. This is a sign that the nervous system is calming down and beginning to release its stored adrenaline charge. It helps us do what animals in the wild naturally do with stress: release it.

The second effect of this exercise is defined by a term I've mentioned previously in this book: Neurosculpting.® I first came up with the term in an attempt to succinctly and precisely describe the process I taught my clients. It is the process by which one targets specific content to be discharged and begins rewriting the nervous system's hold on that pattern. The sculpting process happens through intention, focused imagery, willingness, daily practice, and a nutritionally and mentally primed environment. For me, this effect was the empowerment piece—the practice that taught me I had control of much more than I was taught to believe.

I like to refer to these techniques as navigation tools or maintenance exercises. Each technique is designed to be used over and over for the rest of your life as a means of bringing you back to equilibrium each time there's imbalance. There's really no right or wrong way to use this program, nor is there a correct number of times per month, week, or day to practice the exercises. This resource doesn't come with a prescription—it is designed to elicit your own sense of mastery, navigation, and control so you begin trusting in your own abilities.

I often give this example in my workshops: It's just like brushing your teeth. You don't brush your teeth once when you're a child and you're good to go for the rest of your life. You brush your teeth regularly, because it's preventative maintenance. Some days you definitely feel the need to brush a bit more—like when you've smoked too many cigarettes or had too much coffee or garlic bread and anchovies. You know those times you need a little extra attention to your hygiene, and if you are blissfully unaware of it, others may let you know. You may not be able to explain the chemical process that happens between fluoride and enamel or exactly why your breath is worse some days than others. This lack of scientific understanding doesn't prevent you from brushing your teeth—you simply know and trust that it's a good thing to do for yourself.

Grounding is very similar. Once you begin this practice you will begin identifying times when you are more grounded than others. You will recognize, sometimes late in the game, that it would have helped if you had been grounded during the week. Sometimes others may let you know you are not yourself or are stressed out. You don't need to tax your brain trying to understand exactly how this process works; you only need to do it and the results will become evident. The technique becomes a tool, a reference point, a place to go back to, and a place to prepare from.

One of the things I find so special about these techniques is that I often get information and clarity about some of my very subtle mental states. I will give examples of how to get some of this information a bit later on. Unlike with "no thought" meditation, these techniques are very mind-active. I often have clients start a session by telling me they can't meditate because they can't shut off their thoughts. I don't ask them to. These techniques allow us to create visuals with the mind's eye and to weave intricate and detailed stories for the brain to latch on to. Remember with **Name It and Tame It** that the amygdala calms down when it's in observer mode. Creating visual stories puts us in observer mode, at which point we can begin to step out of the story and watch it. Studies over the past twenty years have shown that during mind-active meditations, individuals can access gamma brain waves and increase their dopamine levels. Since dopamine is basically one of our "feel good, learn well" neurotransmitters, mind-active meditation is associated with increasing one's sense of well-being and capacity to learn new things.

The first presentation of the exercise in each chapter is simply a generic relaxation and release exercise. The second presentation notes ways in which you can target specific content in order to get more information about some of your own subtle programming. This deeper dive is your opportunity to explore interoception.

NOTE: You may want to use a guided recording. You can record yourself reading the meditation scripts and play it back when you want to do the exercises on your own. Give yourself time between each prompt to allow yourself to create the imagery or notice the subtleties. Don't rush. You need not actually *see* anything with your eyes closed! You can simply pretend all of this and you will be able to do the exercise. Remember, your limbic brain doesn't literally see things when you dream, nor does it know the difference between pretend and actuality.

Grounding for Relaxation and Release

1. Begin in a comfortable seat.

2. Clasp your hands together normally, fingers intertwined. Now reverse that clasp by making sure the opposite index finger and thumb are on top. This will likely feel awkward or strange. Keep your hands clasped this way during the breathing portion of the meditation, at which point you are free to unclasp afterwards if you like.

3. Breathe deeply for a few minutes.
   a. Notice how the breath feels entering in through the nose and going down the throat.
   b. Notice how your hands and fingers feel in this position.
   c. Notice how the chair supports your body.
   d. Notice how your bones get heavy.
   e. Notice the temperature on your skin.

4. Locate the base of your spine.
   a. Perhaps you feel this spot.
   b. Perhaps you have an image of this spot.
   c. Maybe you just pretend you've located this spot.

5. Elongate the spine directly out from the body, as though you are growing an extension: a grounding cord.
    a. Notice if you imagine this as a spinal column.
    b. Notice if you imagine this as a tail of some sort.
    c. Notice if you imagine this as a cord or structure of some type.

6. Direct the grounding cord to penetrate through . . .
    a. First, the chair . . .
    b. Next, the floor . . .
    c. Then, the ground . . .
    d. Finally, the earth, all the way until it reaches the earth's core.

7. Notice what the imagery of the center of the earth looks like, as this will be the place best able to receive whatever you will release and give to it.
    a. Perhaps it's molten . . .
    b. Maybe it's a room . . .
    c. It may even be a landscape.

8. Fasten the base of the grounding cord into the center of the earth.
    a. Perhaps it grows roots to root in . . .
    b. Maybe it anchors in . . .
    c. You may even nail it down or plug it in.

9. Paint the cord a color that feels good to you.
    a. Notice what that feels like.

10. Put the current date on the outside of the cord.
    a. Maybe you carve it in . . .
    b. Perhaps you paint it on . . .
    c. Maybe you don't know the date and simply write "present time" or "now."

11. Make the cord wide, perhaps as wide as your hips.

12. Create an on-switch at the top of the cord.
    a. Maybe this is a button . . .
    b. Maybe this looks like a dial . . .
    c. Perhaps this is a lever.

13. Turn the cord on and engage it.

14. Send physical or mental stress, or anything you are ready to be rid of, directly down the cord and out of your body and space.
    a.   Perhaps those are vague sensations.
    b.   Maybe those are specific images.
    c.   Those may be emotions or thoughts.
    d.   Maybe you put individuals down that cord.

15. Sit in this grounded space for a few minutes, noticing what this is like.

16. Bring your awareness back to your breath for a few minutes as you allow your mind to wake back up to your surroundings.

17. Note how you feel now, compared to before you started the exercise.

Make notes in your dedicated journal of any insights, sensations, thoughts, connections, or experiences.

GROUNDING FOR CLARITY AND INFORMATION

1.   Begin in a comfortable seat.

2.   Clasp your hands together normally, fingers intertwined. Now reverse that clasp by making sure the opposite index finger and thumb are on top. This will likely feel awkward or strange. Keep your hands clasped this way during the breathing portion of the meditation, at which point you are free to unclasp afterwards if you like.

3.   Breathe deeply for a few minutes.
    a.   Notice how the breath feels entering in through the nose and going down the throat.
    b.   Notice how your hands and fingers feel in this position.
    c.   Notice how the chair supports your body.
    d.   Notice how your bones get heavy.
    e.   Notice the temperature on your skin.

4. Locate the base of your spine.
   a. Perhaps you feel this spot.
   b. Perhaps you have an image of this spot.
   c. Maybe you just pretend you've located this spot.
   d. Notice your thoughts, images, or associations as you focus on this region of your body.

5. Elongate the spine directly out from the body, as though you are growing an extension: a grounding cord.
   a. Imagine this first as a spinal column.
   b. Next, imagine this as a tail of some sort.
   c. Then, imagine this as a cord or structure of some type.
   d. Notice your preferences and aversions and any associations that might come up with each different cord including thoughts, emotions, and sensation.

6. Direct the grounding cord to penetrate through . . .
   a. First, the chair . . .
   b. Next, the floor . . .
   c. Then, the ground . . .
   d. Finally, the earth, all the way until it reaches the earth's core.

7. Notice what the imagery of the center of the earth looks like, as this will be the place best able to receive whatever you will release and give to it.
   a. First, make it molten.
   b. Next, make it a room.
   c. Then, make it a landscape.
   d. Notice preferences, aversions, and specifically which location makes you feel able to give it your "stuff."

8. Fasten the base of the grounding cord into the center of the earth.
   a. Perhaps it grows roots to root in.
   b. Maybe it anchors in.
   c. You may even nail it down or plug it in.

    d.   Give it a tug to notice what it's like to feel attached.

    e.   If your attachment is weak, change the cord or the way you've attached it.

    f.   Notice the factors that enable the strong attachment.

9. Paint the cord a color.
    a.   First, black.
    b.   Next, yellow.
    c.   Then, the color of safety.
    d.   Lastly, a color that feels good to you.
    e.   Notice preferences, aversions, and any associations or thoughts that come up with each color.

10. Put the current date on the outside of the cord.
    a.   Notice first if there's a date already appearing on your cord.
    b.   Erase any pre-existing date.
    c.   Maybe you carve in the date.
    d.   Perhaps you paint it on.
    e.   Maybe you don't know the date and simply write "present time" or "now."
    f.   Notice any shifts, associations, or thoughts that come up with the current date.

11. Make the cord wide, perhaps as wide as your hips.

12. Create an on-switch at the top of the cord.
    a.   Maybe this is a button . . .
    b.   Maybe this looks like a dial . . .
    c.   Perhaps this is a lever.

13. Turn the cord on and engage it.

14. Send mental or physical stress, or anything you are ready to be rid of, directly down the cord and out of your body and space.
    a.   Send anything that's not in present time down the cord, like vague energies, associations, thoughts, memories, or imagery.
    b.   Send the image of a specific situation down the cord and notice what happens.

   c.   Send physical pain down the cord and notice what happens.

   d.   Send others' information that's not yours down the cord (like opinions and judgments), and notice what happens.

   e.   Send the **I AM** statements you wrote in the **Qualities I Resist** column from Exercise 1 down the cord and notice what happens.

   f.   Notice any body responses—either physical, emotional, or mental—as you send each item down the cord.

   g.   Notice where you have more space.

   h.   Notice where you have resistance to releasing certain topics.

15. Sit in this grounded space for a few minutes noticing what this is like.

16. Bring your awareness back to your breath for a few minutes as you allow your mind to wake back up to your surroundings.

Make notes in your dedicated journal of any insights, sensations, thoughts, connections, or experiences.

In the deeper dive you may have noticed specific reactions as you interacted with more specific imagery. You might have noticed preferences to imagery or even resistance to letting some things go. Perhaps you noticed some thoughts or images arise when you released your **I AM** statements. Maybe you even noticed an inaccurate date already on your cord, indicating you were stuck in some past or future concern. There is no inherent meaning in any of the colors or imagery; however, there is vast personal meaning to *your* limbic brain. For example, in the deeper dive, I prompted you to try a cord colored black, yellow, then the color of safety and, finally, a color you like. Did you notice a preference, or at least a difference? Was the color you chose to represent safety either yellow or black? Maybe so, but likely, not. This is a great example of subtle associations the amygdala has with certain colors. I cannot tell you that your cord *must* be red and then expect you to find a sense of release if red brings up traumatic or negative associations for you consciously or subconsciously for your amygdala. Only you can find what works for you: your brain has all the information you need to best get it to open, release, and relax your body.

This exercise is your playground—a space in which you get to have direct communication with a part of your brain that loves vivid stories and emotional charge. You get to bypass the neocortex logic space and knock directly on the door of the limbic brain and ask the question, "What do you need in order to calm down?" If you ask, it will give you answers! Did you notice differences in imagery, associations, or physical responses as you dumped different aspects down the cord? You need not know what all of those mean. If you are registering anything at all, then your subconscious mind is communicating with you—whether it's through certain resistance to releasing things, certain readiness, effortful distraction, or visceral response. You may be ready to let some things go more easily than others. Some things may have more layers to tend to. You will get this information if you ask for it, as long as you are paying attention to how the creative process of storytelling unfolds.

The more you use this technique, the more you will discover information about your own body-mind associations, stored resistances, and stories.

Suggested Use:

Ground at night to clear out the day's events.

Ground in the morning.

Ground before a potentially stressful event or encounter.

Ground after a stressful event or encounter.

Ground whenever you feel you have a need to release or whenever you feel "full" of stuff that you don't want.

Chapter 10

NEUTRAL SPACE

There truly is no black and white. Mental states are subjective. We each have our own interpretation of what it's like to be neutral. Some people define neutrality as an apathetic approach to all that's going on around them. Some might view neutrality as a passive acceptance of the actions of others or even as a passive way to condone things to which you may be opposed. Still others might define neutrality as an emotional flatness or type of emotional censorship. Many define neutrality as a diplomatic approach to not taking sides.

I don't define it in any of those terms. My version of neutrality launches from this question: Can you put aside your filters, expectations, and beliefs in order to see, feel, experience, and be aware of *all* that is going on around you? If so, then you are neutral according to my definition. Remember, the audience had an expectation of what they would see and fixed attention on a future goal while watching the gorilla-basketball video. They weren't neutral, and because of this few saw the gorilla. In my version of neutrality, emotional expression and experiences are fine—as long as they are in response to what is *actually* going on rather than what one *projects* is going on around him.

It is unrealistic to believe we can be perfectly neutral all the time, but the practice of removing one's filters opens up a much larger field of vision— both figuratively and literally. What could you notice or recognize in your life if you had fewer filters to look through? What opportunities have you missed because your expectations didn't allow you to identify them? What could you notice about your partner, your parents, or your children that you simply couldn't see before? What could you notice about your own actions, patterns, and motivations if your blinders were lifted? What gorilla or elephant is standing in front of *you*?

There are many benefits to creating a neutral space where one goes to experience perceptions beyond those filters. At first when I learned this technique, I had the feeling that I was on some magical vacation. It was a very enticing exercise, and I found myself wanting to go there often. Best of all, this vacation was free! It brought me peace of mind and relaxation. A great benefit of this exercise is that it sets up a reference point for what neutrality feels like versus what it feels like to look through charged filters. It gives one permission to disconnect from judgment and analysis—two great skills of our left brain. It encourages a witness mode or third-party observer framework. This observational framework is critical in the traumatic release technique I mentioned earlier called **Name It and Tame It.** Additionally, this observational mode of meditation has been correlated to lower rates of depression, increased immune functioning, and lower levels of cortisol. I found it liberating to be able to go to a place to *look* at my actions without having to *relive* my actions.

Some individuals believe this is a type of responsibility deferral—that if one doesn't relive their pain, they won't learn from it. For me it was the exact opposite. This exercise caused me to take more responsibility, as I was able to look at my actions much longer and much more deeply when I wasn't battling the debilitating emotions that came with it. I viewed myself or situations from this neutral space and decided to make adjustments to my relationship to that event. From that point, I was much more adept at navigating the emotions of it in a healthy way. I gained an ability to recognize my vices and shortcomings in a way that empowered me to make apologies to wronged individuals, repair some relationship rifts, and recognize others' strengths without being threatened.

Think about it this way: I'm offering you a free vacation to the most amazing place you could ever go, any time you want, and you'll reap major health benefits by going. Tell me, why *wouldn't* you want to go? The only reasons I can think of are that maybe it's unfamiliar and that it requires ten minutes of your time. Do those reasons outweigh the benefits? Can you really afford to pass on this opportunity?

CREATING A NEUTRAL SPACE FOR RELAXATION AND BETTER HEALTH

1. Begin in a comfortable seat.

2. Clasp your hands together normally, fingers intertwined. Now reverse that clasp by making sure the opposite index finger and thumb are on top. This will likely feel awkward or strange. Keep your hands clasped this way during the breathing portion of the meditation, at which point you are free to unclasp afterwards if you like.

3. Breathe deeply for a few minutes.
    a. Notice how the breath feels entering in through the nose and going down the throat.
    b. Notice how your hands and fingers feel in this position.
    c. Notice how the chair supports your body.
    d. Notice how your bones get heavy.
    e. Notice the temperature on your skin.

4. Locate the center of your skull in the middle of your brain.
    a. Perhaps you feel this spot.
    b. Perhaps you have an image of this spot.
    c. Maybe you just pretend you've located this spot.

5. Create the perfect sanctuary here.
    a. Maybe it looks like a room containing all of your favorite objects.
    b. Perhaps it is a landscape you've visited or always wanted to visit.
    c. It may be a location you've never seen or heard of before.

6. Fill this space with all the details that make this perfect.
    a. Experiment with objects.
    b. Envision appropriate colors.
    c. Notice appealing sounds.

7. Create a trap door that leads out of the room and out of your head for any objects you may want to get rid of. Notice if there are any objects present that look like you didn't choose them out of your own desire. Send them down the trap door.

    a. Get rid of colors you didn't choose.

8. Notice if there are any people, pets, or implications of anyone else in there with you. If so, remove them as well by placing them down the trap door or creating a separate room outside your space for them to wait.

9. Notice what it's like to be in your own sanctuary, by yourself. This may very well be the only space in the universe just for you, alone.

10. As though this space were on hydraulic lifts, envision elevating it a tiny bit inside your head to disengage it from your logic space. Allow this room to float, effortlessly, a little higher than it was before.

11. Sit in this floating sanctuary for a few minutes. If thoughts come up, allow them to float by like clouds as you remain comfortably seated in your sanctuary.

12. Notice how you feel now as compared to how you felt before you began this exercise.

Make notes in your dedicated journal of any insights, sensations, thoughts, connections, or experiences.

CREATING A NEUTRAL SPACE FOR NON-JUDGMENTAL INSIGHT AND AWARENESS

1. Begin in a comfortable seat.

2. Clasp your hands together normally, fingers intertwined. Now reverse that clasp by making sure the opposite index finger and thumb are on top. This will likely feel awkward or strange. Keep your hands clasped this way during the breathing portion of the meditation, at which point you are free to unclasp afterwards if you like.

3. Breathe deeply for a few minutes.
   a. Notice how the breath feels entering in through the nose and going down the throat.
   b. Notice how your hands and fingers feel in this position.
   c. Notice how the chair supports your body.
   d. Notice how your bones get heavy.
   e. Notice the temperature on your skin.

4. Locate the center of your skull in the middle of your brain.
   a. Perhaps you feel this spot.
   b. Perhaps you have an image of this spot.
   c. Maybe you just pretend you've located this spot.
   d. Notice any thoughts, patterns, or associations that arise when you locate this area.

5. Create the perfect sanctuary here.
   a. First, create a room with your favorite objects.
   b. Then try a landscape you've visited or always wanted to visit.
   c. Next, envision a location you've never seen or heard of before.
   d. Notice any preferences, associations, thoughts, or imagery that arise with each location. Settle on the sanctuary that felt the easiest and best to you. Notice aspects of the environment that make it feel this way. Erase the rest.

6. Fill this space with all the details that make it perfect.
   a. Experiment with objects.
   b. Envision appropriate colors.
   c. Notice appealing sounds.

7. Create a trap door that leads out of the room and out of your head for any objects you may want to get rid of. Notice if there are any objects present that look like you didn't choose them out of your own desire. Send them down the trap door
   a. Get rid of colors you didn't choose.
   b. Look for areas of blur or haziness and send them down the trap door.

c.   Imagine putting on glasses that give you superhero vision and ask for any foreign energy—meaning energy that's not your own—to show up. Send this energy or imagery down the trap door. Trust the imagery or vague image implications and interact with them whether they are clear or not.

d.   Envision placing any images or attachment to logic down the trap-door.

8.   Notice if there are any people, pets, or implications of anyone else in there with you. If so, remove them as well by placing them down the trap door or creating a separate room outside your space for them to wait.

a.   Notice your ease or reluctance to remove individuals and pets.

b.   Notice the ease or reluctance individuals may express as you imagine removing them.

c.   Notice any associations, thought forms, experiences, or sensations that arise or linger as you remove individuals.

9.   Notice what it's like to be in your own sanctuary, by yourself. This may very well be the only space in the universe just for you, alone. This is your neutral command center, the place from which conscious creation is possible.

10. Make this space bigger, so the room takes up more of your skull.

a.   Notice the ease or difficulty claiming more space just for you.

b.   Notice any thoughts, associations, patterns, images, or experiences that arise from expanding your neutral space.

11. As though this space were on hydraulic lifts, envision elevating it a tiny bit inside your head to disengage it from your logic space. Allow this room to float, effortlessly, a little higher than is was before.

a.   Notice your ease or reluctance to separate from your logic mind.

12. Sit in this floating sanctuary for a few minutes. If thoughts come up, allow them to float by like clouds as you remain comfortably seated in your sanctuary.

13. Imagine a movie screen in your space and picture watching a movie just beyond your closed eyes. Envision yourself as the main character in the movie.

    a. Observe the character as it embodies or acts out each of the **I AM** statements you wrote in the **Qualities I Resist** column from Exercise I. As the image acts out a statement, notice what that looks like.

    b. Watch the image disappear or melt away as you create the next image of yourself embodying the next **I AM** statement.

    c. Repeat until all the **I AM** statements have been represented and observed.

14. Notice your experience of **watching** the images versus your experience of what it was like to initially write the **I AM** statements.

15. Envision the end of the movie and just enjoy being in your sanctuary with nothing to do.

16. Notice how you feel now as compared to before you began this exercise.

Make notes in your dedicated journal of any insights, sensations, thoughts, connections, or experiences.

In this deeper dive, you may have noticed a different experience in your body when you thought of your **I AM** statements than the experience you had when you first wrote the list. You may have perceived certain individuals in your life laying claim to your head space, possibly even resistant to leaving. Some people may experience guilt as they attempt to clear their space. If the aspect of neutrality is new to you, you may have even noticed a bit of apprehension around claiming space for yourself, as though you needed permission from someone or something. Some of you may have even noticed patterns or beliefs rising to the surface as you observed your **I AM** statements from neutrality.

There is no need to attach thoughts to this process such as, "Did I do it right?" or "That's not good." There's not even a real need to understand or even remember the imagery that comes up. The opportunity you have with this exercise is to allow relational information to present itself to you in a way that doesn't require you to engage with it. If you watch it and don't engage with it, then you are in witness mode. Remember, when we relive our thoughts, memories, and beliefs, we easily activate our stress response. This is an occasion in which you give your beliefs space and permission to come up and move on without engaging old neural circuitry, hormonal reaction, or chemical and electrical firing.

The more you create a situation in which you practice being the observer, the more you gain a reference point for what that feels like. Did *watching* the **I AM** representations create a different experience for you than *labeling* yourself with them in the very first exercise? For each belief you have about yourself, there exists neural patterns that activate, reinforcing that belief with physical response each time you think it. This is your golden opportunity to create a new neural path—one that engages a different response, as you observe certain beliefs from your neutral space. The more you observe from this space, the more you create new thought patterns, associations, and neural pathways. These become alternative pathways to the default options that bound you to old beliefs. Not only are you sculpting new pathways by practicing this exercise, but within the exercise you also have the opportunity to sculpt new imagery. The power of creation here is limitless.

Suggested Use:

Every day as part of your morning or evening routine.

Any time you feel you need a vacation.

Any time a situation or relationship elicits a patterned response you are trying to break.

Any time you want to look at a stressful situation without reliving it.

Any time you feel heavily influenced and pressured.

Before going in to a volatile situation—you can try staying in that neutral space during the situation.

Just after a volatile situation to change your perspective.

Chapter 11

PERSONAL BOUNDARIES

It's amazing to me that every time I introduce this topic to officers, I get complete agreement—and even adamant support of this concept. I say I'm amazed because it's one of the few times that my most left-brained audiences fully support unsubstantiated and subjective information: the concept of personal space—our individual sphere of activity. We all have different comfort levels with personal space. In the United States, most people's personal space radiates about arms' length out from their bodies. Of course, this varies from person to person. In some professions, such as law enforcement, an officer wouldn't want strangers to get that close, as it represents danger. Different countries and cultures have different perceptions of personal space. In some cultures, physical proximity during conversations can be very close. To Americans, that might be uncomfortable. Think about those encounters you've had where a stranger leans in very close, talking to you with less than six inches separating your faces. How did that make you feel? What was your comfort level? How did you react? I had a friend when I was younger who had a completely different comfort level than I did with personal space. Whenever we'd talk, she'd put her face much closer to mine than I was used to. I found myself positioning one of my legs in front of my body, leaning back a bit, with my arms crossed in front of me. The more I leaned back, the more she leaned in. I had no real explanation for this sense of having my space invaded—she was neither a stranger nor threatening. Yet something in me felt that such proximity was just too close.

Think about the following questions to get a better sense of your relationship to this concept.

If you were the only person in an elevator and someone else got on, would you be comfortable if they stood next to you, shoulders touching? Would you be comfortable if that person stood six inches away? Twelve inches? Two feet?

If you entered a movie theater and it was empty, except for one person sitting in the back, would you choose the seat right next to that one person? How many seats or rows would you need between you and the other person to feel comfortable?

How comfortable would you be if someone got in line behind you at a store and their toes touched the backs of your heels or you felt their breath in your hair or on the back of your neck? How far away must a stranger behind you stand in order for you to be comfortable?

Your responses to these questions are in direct relationship to *your* definition of personal space. This invisible bubble in which we encapsulate ourselves is unique to each of us, adjustable based on our environment, as much a part of us as our limbs, and highly attuned to its own boundaries. It's so sensitive, in fact, that sometimes you can feel when someone is staring at you from behind. Have you ever had the perception of being watched, only to turn around and find out you were correct?

Each of us living organisms has a magnetic field resonating around us. We can tune in to this magnetic field and use it to "feel" things even though they are invisible—like the person glaring at you from behind. Let me give you an even more practical example. Let's say your day was perfect: easy commute, effortless production at work, good lunch, and great weather. Your drive home was great too—good music and no traffic. You enter your home and you are greeted by an angry, pessimistic, blaming, and accusatory partner, who happened to have the worst day possible. How long does it typically take for you to lose your great feeling and adopt a cruddy attitude? Sometimes this happens in just a few seconds.

This is an example of someone else's attitude—or even magnetic resonance—sitting in your space. Not only is it sitting there uninvited, but you are now acting upon it as though it were yours. You match your mood to it, even though nothing actually happened to *you* during your day to cause this mood. We know the result of too much stress on our psyche and our health, so why compound the situation by carrying other people's stress as well? Since each of us must interact with the world, there's no way to prevent this sort of energy exchange, but there *is* a way to identify some of what's in your personal space. You can begin to recognize how well defined your boundaries are, and you can even develop a process for clearing your space and regaining balance. We can't coat ourselves with Teflon, but we can enhance our awareness in order to maintain well-being and clarity. We have the ability to determine what we want to keep in our sphere of activity.

In actuality, our brains begin reacting to what our senses detect *before* we are ever conscious of what's going on. We subconsciously react to various subtle energies in our close proximity all the time. Have you ever felt the hair on the back of your neck stand up *before* you were conscious of a threat behind you? I had an amazing experience of identifying things in my personal space in my wilderness survival course at Tracker School (an experience I highly recommend to everyone!). This was an awareness exercise. The tracker led a group into the woods at night. It was difficult to see with our eyes open, as there was no moon, and we were in the thick brush of a cedar swamp. One by one, he blindfolded us. About a quarter of a mile away, in a place we hadn't been to before, was a man sitting by a campfire, banging a drum at slow and easy intervals. Our task: to navigate through the woods and make it to the man with the drum without using our eyes. We could take as long as necessary.

I am not ashamed to say it's unnerving to stand alone in the woods, blindfolded in the dark. There's a vulnerability that arises that typically puts one in threat mode. It takes internal negotiation to remove the fear component and trust in an inherent ability to navigate. The group scattered, and I found myself frightened and quite clumsy. The brush was cumbersome, thorny, and quite high in certain areas. I walked with my arms out in front of me, flailing a bit, feeling much like the Bride of Frankenstein. There were many times I lost my balance and grabbed onto bushes to hold me up. I laughed and got a little sad at the way I felt so alien to nature. On a few occasions, I bumped right into trees. This is about when total humility kicked in. I was overwhelmed with new stimuli and confused about what to pay attention to: the drum, the sound of crackling leaves, the feel of the terrain, animal sounds, wind, and each little insect. Sadly, I was overwhelmed *without* the distraction of technology, my eyes, and our usual false sense of control.

Finally, after much effort and very little grace, I decided to relax. I stopped . . . breathed deeply . . . yielded to darkness . . . created a grounding cord . . . and listened for the drum. I began fox-walking—the kind of gait trackers use to make no sound and connect with the earth. At the moment I slowed down, I noticed something I hadn't before—something that was there all the time. I could *sense* when there was a tree or limb in front of me *before* I encountered it. My best description of that knowing comes from a combination of sensory experiences, only some of which I can describe. The air shifted—thickening in front of me. Sound became insulated, as though my head were lying on a sandy beach. There was a perception of height approaching, although I have no idea how to describe that sensation. I'd feel a presence very near me, stronger as I approached.

I tested myself. If I felt there was a tree in front of me or a limb out to my left, I'd place my hands where I perceived. I was right, every time. But I could only detect this when I was slow, relaxed, and aware of what was in my personal space—my sphere of activity. The minute I shifted into my logic brain to analyze where the next tree *should* be, I'd lose the sensation. As the trees entered my personal space, I detected them *without* my eyes and *before* my body made contact.

This is exactly the skill we all have. It doesn't need to be a tree in your space to recognize something is there. Imagine how handy it would be to identify what subtle attitudes or energies Ping-Pong us around, affecting our moods on a whim, making us feel tossed-about by life.

Whether the energies are subtle or quite pronounced, like someone's foul mood, our space collects and reacts to all that enters it. This technique is designed to give you a way to remove that and get clarity about what collects in that space.

PERSONAL BOUNDARIES FOR RELAXATION AND RELEASE

1. Begin in a comfortable seat.

2. Clasp your hands together normally, fingers intertwined. Now reverse that clasp by making sure the opposite index finger and thumb are on top. This will likely feel awkward or strange. Keep your hands clasped this way during the breathing portion of the meditation, at which point you are free to unclasp afterwards if you like.

3. Breathe deeply for a few minutes.
   a. Notice how the breath feels entering in through the nose and going down the throat.
   b. Notice how your hands and fingers feel in this position.
   c. Notice how the chair supports your body.
   d. Notice how your bones get heavy.
   e. Notice the temperature on your skin.

4. Imagine you are floating in the center of a bubble.
   a. Notice how large the bubble is.
   b. Notice the space above your head, between you and the bubble.
   c. Notice the space below your feet, between you and the bubble.

5. Set the size of the bubble to be about one arm's-length out from your body on all sides.
   a. Notice if you have a sense of making the bubble larger to accomplish this.
   b. Notice if you have a sense of making the bubble smaller to accomplish this.

6. Create a grounding cord for the bubble that connects at the bottom of the bubble and goes to the center of the earth. You may also decide to use your existing grounding cord to attach to the bubble. Use all the same steps to create the bubble's grounding cord as you did for your own.

7. Imagine releasing any energy that doesn't belong to you from inside the bubble, right down the grounding cord.
   a. Perhaps you imagine a color to represent yourself and look for any other color in the bubble in addition to your own.

8. Float in the cleared-out bubble and notice any sensations, thoughts, associations, or experiences

9. Choose a color to represent you and fill the bubble with that color.
   a. Maybe it pours in through the top.
   b. Perhaps you envision it being sprayed in or painted.
   c. You may perceive that it just appears.

10. Bring your awareness back to your breath for a few minutes as you allow your mind to wake back up to your surroundings.

11. Note how you feel now compared to how you felt before you started the exercise.

Make notes in your dedicated journal of any insights, sensations, thoughts, connections, or experiences.

PERSONAL BOUNDARIES FOR SELF-REFERENCE AND CLARITY

1. Begin in a comfortable seat.

2. Clasp your hands together normally, fingers intertwined. Now reverse that clasp by making sure the opposite index finger and thumb are on top. This will likely feel awkward or strange. Keep your hands clasped this way during the breathing portion of the meditation, at which point you are free to unclasp afterwards if you like.

3. Breathe deeply for a few minutes.
   a. Notice how the breath feels entering in through the nose and going down the throat.
   b. Notice how your hands and fingers feel in this position.
   c. Notice how the chair supports your body.
   d. Notice how your bones get heavy.
   e. Notice the temperature on your skin.

4. Imagine you are floating in the center of a bubble.
   a. Notice how large the bubble is.
   b. Notice the space above your head, between you and the bubble.
   c. Notice the space below your feet, between you and the bubble.
   d. Notice any thoughts, experiences, or associations that arise.

5. Set the size of the bubble to be about one arm's-length out from your body on all sides.
   a. Notice if you have a sense of making the bubble larger to accomplish this.
   b. Notice if you have a sense of making the bubble smaller to accomplish this.
   c. Observe your experience of being inside this size space.
   d. Observe if it's comforting or unsettling to set your bubble at this size.
   e. Notice your relationship to taking ownership of your space.

6. Choose a color you like, and imagine painting the outer boundary of this bubble that color to mark it clearly.
   a. Notice your experience of being in the center of a bubble with a clearly marked boundary.

7. Create a grounding cord for the bubble that connects at the bottom of the bubble and goes to the center of the earth. You may also decide to use your existing grounding cord to attach to the bubble. Use all the same steps to create the bubble's grounding cord as you did for your own.

8. Imagine releasing any foreign energy from the bubble, right down the grounding cord.
   a. Choose a color to represent your family and imagine releasing that energy out of the bubble.
   b. Choose a color to represent your work or profession and release that energy out of the bubble.
   c. Choose a color to represent any institution to which you may belong and release that energy out of the bubble.
   d. Run through each of the **I AM** statements and imagine releasing each of them from your bubble.
   e. Assign colors to any other concepts you wish and release them from your bubble.
   f. Notice your experience of releasing those colors and of being in that bubble without them.

9. Float in the cleared-out bubble and notice any sensations, thoughts, associations, or experiences.

10. Choose a color to represent your own essence and fill the bubble in with that color
    a. Maybe you have it pour in through the top.
    b. Perhaps you envision is being sprayed on or painted.
    c. You may perceive that it just appears.

11. Bring your awareness back to your breath for a few minutes as you allow your mind to wake back up to your surroundings.

12. Note how you feel now compared to how you felt before you started the exercise.

Make notes in your dedicated journal of any insights, sensations, thoughts, connections, or experiences.

In this deeper dive, you might have noticed your ease or difficulty in releasing some of your **I AM** statements from your personal space. Perhaps you even noticed which ones took up more room than others. Some of you might have even registered varying comfort levels once the **I AM** statements were not active in your bubble. In some cases, you may have noticed a vulnerability, while in others, you might notice a sense of relief. These observations are specific to you. You can continue experimenting with the **I AM** statements and over time you might notice a different relationship emerging with each of them.

I have had lots of fun and received many insights by using this exercise, in addition to lots of healing. There have been times where work stressed me in such a way that I couldn't stop the spillover into my personal life. In these times I'd use this exercise, only to realize my bubble was full of energy or concepts that belonged to someone or something else. Giving myself permission to clear that out of my space offered a sense of freedom and healthy separation. I was able to gauge the integrity of my actions when I was full of external influences versus my actions when I cleared out my space. The powerful aspect of this exercise for me has been that I gained a clear sense of what it feels like to be in my own space, free of others' "stuff." This enables me, and will enable you, to identify when even the smallest influence enters the bubble and begins to affect thoughts and behavior. Imagine it this way: If your room were dirty, unorganized, and overflowing, how easy would it be to notice a paperclip thrown into the middle of it all? How easy would it be to notice that paperclip if the room had been clean and organized to start with? This is only one of the benefits of this exercise. The more you clear, the quicker and easier you notice when it gets dirty. We've learned that we tell ourselves counter-productive stories all the time. The last thing we need is for the stories of others to contribute to that momentum.

Suggested Use:

Every day, after the Grounding and Neutral Space exercises.

Any time you feel unclear about your actions or motives.

Before going to work or being social.

After intense interactions.

Daily, if you spend lots of time with the same people each day.

Any time you feel reactive, defensive, or charged.

Chapter 12

FILLING IN

If we look at the first three exercises sequentially, here's what you've accomplished: You initiated and created a parasympathetic state by grounding; you stepped away from judgment of the left brain, and gained a neutral perspective by creating and attending to your head space; and finally, you cleared energy and external influences from your personal space by gaining awareness of your boundaries. This is amazing! Think of all the expansion and release your nervous system experienced. For some of you, this may even be the most time you've ever spent nurturing yourself from the inside out. Congratulations!

The good news is, there's more! To introduce this next exercise I'm going to switch gears and discuss the mundane. No matter what our station in life is, we all seem to have a common denominator of household chores: cleaning the dishes, throwing out moldy food from the refrigerator, and cleaning the closets. It astounds me that I can spend an entire afternoon cleaning and organizing such a small area of my house. As I sift through piles of things, it's as though old items I can't let go of resurface, inextricably intertwined with new items I have no recollection of buying or even needing. Such are the perils of having a deep closet. After you've spent your valuable time on this chore, how long does it take for you to mess up the closet again? If you're like me, it takes about two days. This closet phenomenon is equally as enigmatic, and as prevalent, as the renegade sock-in-the-laundry mystery. I'm guessing (like many of you) that I might have found a halfway decent solution. I added organizers and drawers to the open space in my closet, and that seems to help a bit. I still find ways of filling the in-between spaces with junk, but with respect to the new organizing structure I put in my closet, these piles are now much smaller.

Each of us varies in our ability to stay clear and organized, but inevitably, the mess happens, and we need to clean the closet again. Our state of mind is no different. Everything you've released in your grounding and clearing exercises made room for more *stuff* to fill in. Like restructuring a newly cleaned closet, this exercise intentionally and decisively fills in that space before other, more unsavory things find root there. This exercise enables us to create a new foundation of functionality, one that is imbued with the emotional associations we *choose*. Remember, our limbic brain kicks in when our experiences are matched to stored stories with associated emotional fear. You now have the means and opportunity to write some new stories and to choose the emotional charge you want associated with it.

As we continue to create stories in our lives, many of which are mapped against past experiences and projected to future scenarios, we leave pieces of ourselves in those snapshots. As we invest our neurology into a story, it holds a piece of us at that time, embedded in the workings of that particular neurological network. I know this just as you know this—from the fact that you can have a story lay dormant for years and still relive it with a visceral emotional experience at a later date. The reliving is not mapped to new emotions but to the very ones you felt at the *moment in time* you had the experience. So in a very real sense, you are visiting a piece of yourself stamped in a time other than the present moment. Imagine the vast amount of energy and resources we spend allocating pieces of ourselves to the myriad memories and plans we create. These pieces of ourselves would serve us much better if we reclaimed them from those stories and brought them into our experience of the here and now. Imagine having many of your emotional resources, which have been spread thin, suddenly available to you. We *can* reclaim doled-out pieces of ourselves allocated to stories of the past.

Biologically, we are not the same people today that we were yesterday. Cells die and are replaced throughout our entire body all the time. So why should we view our neurology and thoughts any differently? The brain is plastic in its ability to rewire and remap. Our thoughts are a major mechanism in the brain's remapping strategy. In fact, we're subconsciously remapping all the time. It's time to get smart and intentional about how we sculpt our realities, and this exercise is a powerful way to do so. Choice is one of our greatest human traits. Conscious choice, applied to how we perceive the world, is the next wave of our personal evolution. This also happens to be the exercise that usually makes my clients feel a sense of bliss, although that is not a prescribed result.

FILLING IN FOR RELAXATION AND WELL-BEING

1. Begin in a comfortable seat.

2. Clasp your hands together normally, fingers intertwined. Now reverse that clasp by making sure the opposite index finger and thumb are on top. This will likely feel awkward or strange. Keep your hands clasped this way during the breathing portion of the meditation, at which point you are free to unclasp afterwards if you like.

3. Breathe deeply for a few minutes.
   a. Notice how the breath feels entering in through the nose and going down the throat.
   b. Notice how your hands and fingers feel in this position.
   c. Notice how the chair supports your body.
   d. Notice how your bones get heavy.
   e. Notice the temperature on your skin.

4. Imagine a huge receptacle or gold sun hovering above your head.
   a. Perhaps you pretend this is there.
   b. Maybe you sense this.
   c. You might have an image of this.

5. Envision a magnet in the center of this sun which attracts your own energy. Imagine any of your own energy flowing into this sun from anywhere you might have left it outside of yourself.

    a.   Perhaps you have a vague image of this happening.

    b.   Maybe you notice where your energy is streaming in from.

6. When the sun is full imagine you have a seed of a thought or intention that you are about to throw into the sun. Choose a concept or thought for this seed.

    a.   Perhaps it's trust.

    b.   Maybe it's joy.

    c.   It may be anything you desire.

7. Watch the seed expand and grow until it fills the entire sun, which is now brimming with your own reclaimed energy mixed with the energy of your chosen intention.

8. Imagine this energy spilling out and pouring into the top of your head.

    a.   Fill in your entire body.

    b.   Notice it filling in your muscles.

    c.   Notice it filling in your cells.

9. Once your body is full, allow this energy to spill out the bottoms of your feet and fill in all the space of the bubble you made earlier.

    a.   Notice your experience of being full and floating in this particular image.

10. Note how you feel now compared to before you started the exercise.

Make notes in your dedicated journal of any insights, sensations, thoughts, connections, or experiences.

FILLING IN FOR INFORMATION AND DISCOVERY

1. Begin in a comfortable seat.

2. Clasp your hands together normally, fingers intertwined. Now reverse that clasp by making sure the opposite index finger and thumb are on

top. This will likely feel awkward or strange. Keep your hands clasped this way during the breathing portion of the meditation, at which point you are free to unclasp afterwards if you like.

3. Breathe deeply for a few minutes.
   a. Notice how the breath feels entering in through the nose and going down the throat.
   b. Notice how your hands and fingers feel in this position.
   c. Notice how the chair supports your body.
   d. Notice how your bones get heavy.
   e. Notice the temperature on your skin.

4. Imagine a huge receptacle or gold sun hovering above your head.
   a. Perhaps you pretend this is there.
   b. Maybe you sense this.
   c. You might have an image of this.

5. Envision a magnet in the center of this sun which attracts your own energy. Imagine any of your own energy flowing into this sun from anywhere you might have left it.
   a. Ask for your energy to return from certain memories and notice what comes back.
   b. Ask for your energy to return from anyone you may have left it with and observe what shows up.
   c. Ask for your energy to return from any future concerns and notice that experience.
   d. Ask for your energy to return from dreams and observe that experience.
   e. Notice where your energy was held.

6. When the sun is full, imagine you have a seed of a thought or intention that you are about to throw into the sun. Choose a new **I AM** concept or thought for this seed.
   a. Perhaps it's **I AM** trust.
   b. Maybe it's **I AM** joy.
   c. It may be anything you desire.

7. Watch the seed expand and grow until it fills the entire sun, which is now brimming with your own reclaimed energy mixed with the energy of your chosen intention.
    a. Notice the way in which the two energies mix.

8. Imagine this energy spilling out and pouring into the top of your head.
    a. Fill in your entire body.
    b. Notice it filling in your muscles.
    c. Notice it filling in your cells.
    d. Observe the areas of the body that need to fill in more and longer than others.
    e. Notice what happens in those areas as you fill in.
    f. Observe any sensory or emotional experiences.

9. Once your body is full, allow this energy to spill out the bottoms of your feet and fill in all the space of the bubble you made earlier.
    a. Notice your experience of being full and floating in this particular image.

10. Note how you feel now compared to before you started the exercise.

Make notes in your dedicated journal of any insights, sensations, thoughts, connections, or experiences.

For this deeper dive you might have noticed that relationships or people from your past popped into your thoughts as you reclaimed your energy. Sometimes old memories or dreams resurface. You may have even noticed a release of emotions or a sense of non-attachment to those images that came up. It's possible in this exercise to notice reactions in parts of your body as you fill in with your own energy. Individuals sometimes note that this exercise makes them feel more like "themselves" than they have in a long time.

I have experienced many different things with this exercise. Often, I fill in with something desirable, so I feel a sense of well-being. Many times I feel full, calm, rejuvenated, and ready to interact with the world with more patience. I have been able to notice specific areas of my body that need to fill in more based on stored stress patterns in my muscles. I have had many insights regarding where I invest my energy based on my ability to reclaim it. I also have the experience of shifting relationship dynamics when I fill in with something desirable before having a potentially volatile interaction. I have filled in with ideas of healing or perfect health and have noticed ailments go away. Conversely, I have filled in with foreign or strange concepts to experiment and have found myself acting out of character during those times. Your experiences will be unique, so be open to noticing how this exercise works for you.

Suggested Use:

After the three previous exercises.

At the beginning or end of each day.

Any time you want to experience a particular intention.

Any time you feel spread thin or exhausted.

When you are locked into an old pattern.

When your body aches.

Any time you are sick.

Whenever it's desirable!

Chapter 13

CLEANSING AND PROGRAMMING

"I admit that thoughts influence the body."

~ Albert Einstein

This exercise is very near and dear to my heart. It is the first meditation exercise I used regularly as a very young meditator, and it was my lifeline through my adolescent years and many turbulent times as a teenager. I first used this exercise to initiate a parasympathetic response in my body. It helped me sleep, made me feel a total buzz during the day, and brought me lots of comfort and joy. I used it at least once a day, sometimes more often. It was a respite for me during times of stress. It gave me confidence during times of confusion. It made me feel connected to something greater. I always felt empowered after this exercise, as though I had just done something very special and healing for myself. I experienced this exercise very viscerally, more so than any of the others. Perhaps that's because it was the first formalized meditation I had engaged in, or perhaps it's simply because there's such a strong somatic imagery involved. In a regular meditation group I teach, this exercise has been claimed as the favorite as well.

Once I was comfortable with the basic process, I added a cognitive-programming component that introduced a level of excitement and intent to the exercise. As a young child I was fascinated with my ability to learn subconsciously. I always believed I could choose a topic before bed and learn about it in my dreams. I was obsessed with books on lucid dreaming, increasing my memory, and the concept of visiting other worlds. I renewed Harry Lorayne's books, *How to Develop a Super-Power Memory* and *Harry Lorayne's Secrets of Mind Power* at least three times from the library when I was in junior high. I totally believed I could reprogram myself.

I wrote in my journal before and after each time I used this meditation, and I tracked how my reality changed. You can use this exercise to set a goal or intention for yourself, prime your mind and body to integrate that goal, and rewire some of your thoughts, so that attaining that goal becomes a reality. However, try not to have expectations about the outcome, because then you put yourself into a mindset that relies on reward or accomplishment. This type of mindset may be good for certain things but with meditation it just engages frustration and disappointment if the reward is not met—and this is exactly the opposite of what you want to do.

Our brains are wired to notice, process, organize, encode, and heal much better during relaxed states than during stressed states. In fact, recent neuroscience studies done at Northwestern and Drexel universities show that seconds before individuals report moments of insight, their brains shift into the alpha brainwave state. This is the state akin to relaxation, and it is easily attained through meditation. Once the brain shifts into alpha patterns, it primes itself to have a burst of gamma waves, which occur at a much higher hertz frequency. The burst of gamma waves is reported to happen precisely at the moment of insight. It is an actual instantaneous synchrony of neurons in the right side of the brain. It is a moment in which neurons in various parts of the brain all fire the same message, at the same time, like a unified bonding experience. Science, it seems, is reporting that this meditation-relaxed state is a precursor for some of these types of higher level brain functioning.

This exercise offered me the simplest and most direct experience of that framework. Whether you want to call it programming, subliminal suggestion, self-hypnosis, or any other title, the end result of this technique was that it was much easier for me to attain certain skills or meet specific goals when I engaged in this practice. I've taught this technique to the meditation groups I facilitate—and it has been received with overwhelming satisfaction. Your experience with this exercise should serve as your own authority.

Cleansing for Space and Relaxation

1. Begin in a comfortable seat.

2. Clasp your hands together normally, fingers intertwined. Now reverse that clasp by making sure the opposite index finger and thumb are on top. This will likely feel awkward or strange. Keep your hands clasped this way during the breathing portion of the meditation, at which point you are free to unclasp afterwards if you like.

3. Breathe deeply for a few minutes.
   a. Notice how the breath feels entering in through the nose and going down the throat.
   b. Notice how your hands and fingers feel in this position.
   c. Notice how the chair supports your body.
   d. Notice how your bones get heavy.
   e. Notice the temperature on your skin.

4. Imagine your body full of tiny scrubbing bubbles from head to toe.
   a. Perhaps this looks like foam.
   b. Maybe this appears as those scrubbing bubbles from the old television commercials.
   c. You might envision these to be tiny sponges or brushes.

5. Imagine the bubbles popping, beginning at your toes. Everywhere they pop they leave an empty and clean space.
   a. Maybe you imagine this as a visual.
   b. Perhaps you actually feel your body's response.

6. Move up your body in small increments until you've popped and cleaned every part of yourself.

a. Perhaps you notice the difference in areas where the bubbles have popped versus areas where they haven't.

b. Maybe you notice a shift in thoughts or images as you pop the bubbles.

7. Once you've popped all the bubbles, imagine yourself floating empty.

a. Perhaps you are floating in space.

b. Maybe you imagine you are floating in water.

8. Bring your attention to your breath and with each inhale imagine you are refilling all of that space with fresh, clean energy.

a. Perhaps you begin filling from your toes.

b. Maybe you imagine your breath filling in from the top of your head.

9. When you are completely full just observe how you feel.

a. Perhaps you notice a body experience.

b. Maybe you notice the nature of your thoughts.

c. You may even perceive where you have more space.

10. Bring your awareness back to your breath for a few minutes as you allow your mind to wake back up to your surroundings.

11. Note how you feel now compared to before you started the exercise.

Make notes in your dedicated journal of any insights, sensations, thoughts, connections, or experiences.

Cleansing for Space, Programming, and Transformation

1. Begin this exercise by looking at some of the **I AM** qualities you are in resistance to. Choose one you'd like to rewrite. For example, if I chose **I AM reactionary**, I might want to rewrite that as **I AM able to see situations from a larger perspective than my own.** You are not restricted to using your **I AM** list. Feel free to write any statement you'd like.

2. Actually write the new statement on an index card. Be as specific as possible in your goal and your time frame for attaining it. Read this statement both out loud and silently a few times, picturing each word clearly in your mind.

3. Sit in a comfortable seat.

4. Clasp your hands together normally, fingers intertwined. Now reverse that clasp by making sure the opposite index finger and thumb are on top. This will likely feel awkward or strange. Keep your hands clasped this way during the breathing portion of the meditation, at which point you are free to unclasp afterwards if you like.

Breathe deeply for a few minutes.

    a. Notice how the breath feels entering in through the nose and going down the throat.

    b. Notice how your hands and fingers feel in this position.

    c. Notice how the chair supports your body.

    d. Notice how your bones get heavy.

    e. Notice the temperature on your skin.

5. Imagine your body full of tiny scrubbing bubbles from head to toe.

    a. Perhaps this looks like foam.

    b. Maybe this appears as those scrubbing bubbles from the old television commercials.

    c. You might envision these to be tiny sponges or brushes.

6. Imagine the bubbles popping, beginning at your toes. Everywhere they pop, they leave an empty and clean space.

    a. Maybe you imagine this as a visual.

    b. Perhaps you actually feel your body's response.

7. Move up your body in small increments until you've popped and cleaned every part of yourself.

    a. Perhaps you notice the difference in areas where the bubbles have popped, versus areas where they haven't.

b. Maybe you notice a shift in thoughts or images as you pop the bubbles.

8. Once you've popped all the bubbles, imagine yourself floating empty.
   a. Perhaps you are floating in space.
   b. Maybe you imagine you are floating in water.

9. Bring your attention to your breath, and with each inhalation, imagine you are refilling all of that space with your rewritten sentence from your index card.
   a. Perhaps you begin filling from your toes.
   b. Maybe you imagine your breath filling in from the top of your head.

10. When you are completely full, just observe how you feel.
    a. Perhaps you notice a body experience.
    b. Maybe you notice the nature of your thoughts.
    c. You may even perceive where you have more space.

11. Bring your awareness back to your breath for a few minutes as you allow your mind to wake back up to your surroundings.

12. Note how you feel now compared to before you started the exercise.

Make notes in your dedicated journal of any insights, sensations, thoughts, connections, or experiences.

For me, having goals involving only my own transformation was important. I was inspired to dedicate myself to my practice because I was intrigued to notice my own progress. At twelve, I had set a goal that I'd get better at math. I did this exercise every night for at least a week before I perceived my math skills were getting better. Tests seemed easier. I doubt this was a normal approach to studying or homework, but it seemed to work for me. I layered many different goals into these exercises. The more incremental progress I made, the more dedicated I became.

Don't try to use these programming techniques to change other people or external situations. They are for you and your own transformation. I highly recommend staying away from an approach in which you are trying to manipulate others' ideas, behaviors, or perceptions. The only true way to elicit any sort of change in the world is to be the example of that change. So, although many external experiences may shift through your use of this technique and others, it's important for the goal to remain focused on your own shift. Remember, we already know how to spend much of our time focused on the outer world of people, places, and things. Don't doubt for a minute that you have the power to be a catalyst for transformation in others—just remember it's a byproduct of *your own* shifting. I have encountered other teaching modalities that involve manipulation of other's perceptions, thoughts, energies, or motivations. And while that may work, it is not the modality I choose to practice or represent in this book. Your written goal will be most effective when it applies specifically to *you*. Additionally, if you start tracking progress and achievement to your own personal growth, your brain will reap wonderful status rewards and release "feel good" neurotransmitters.

Suggested Use:

Every day, at the start or end of the day for clearing.

Any time you want to focus on specific goal accomplishment.

Any time you want to rewrite a pattern, belief, or aspect of your perception.

When you want to feel relaxed.

When you feel stifled, restricted, or stuck.

After difficult interactions.

Before critical conversations.

"Whoever undertakes to set himself up as a judge of Truth and Knowledge is shipwrecked by the laughter of the gods."

~ Albert Einstein

Chapter 14

RIGHT BRAIN–LEFT BRAIN COMMUNICATION

In Part I, we talked about the aspects and attributes of the left and right hemispheres of the brain. Additionally, you did a short exercise in which you began to identify which side of the brain you prefer to use day to day. In this exercise, you get a unique opportunity to visit both sides and create increased communication to and from the areas you may not use as frequently. You get to choose the type of balanced relationship you want between the side that thinks it knows the truth and the side that can experience life differently from that labeled truth. We are comfortable in our defaults—but as we've learned throughout this book, we can be so much more effective in our own healing and transformation when we expand out of our comfort zone.

Imagine having the clarity and ability to notice exactly when one side of the brain could help you engage with the world differently, problem-solve more effectively, encourage insights, and engage an extra set of skills you may not have realized you had. Knowledge is power, but application and practice is the *use* of that power. Stephen Covey once said, "To know and not to do is not to know." What good is your power if you are not using it?

Most of the clients with whom I use this exercise have a default preference for their left brain. If you think about it, it makes sense. Most people come to see me because they are stuck in stress or trauma cycles dictated by their limbic brain. However, it's their left brain that chooses to believe that story as a definition of reality and an association with who they are. So many of my clients are looking for ways to feel joy, expansiveness, oneness, and intuitive insight—in other words, they are seeking to embrace archetypal right-brain qualities. You may be different. Maybe you prefer to use your right brain more day to day. The beauty of this exercise is that you can use it to begin dialogue with either side. It's up to you. Remember, we create neuronal pathways and maps based on what we pay focused attention to. If we default to one map regularly, we strengthen those pathways and convince our brains that "this way" is the only way.

This exercise takes your focused attention and directs it precisely towards the areas you don't default to—creating neuronal activity and mapping where it may not have been before. I created this exercise many years ago and have used many derivations of it since. I've seen this one have instantaneous results in my office with some very traumatized individuals. It is a humbling and amazing thing to witness the childlike look of excitement on a client's face when they experience the reality that they are much more than what their limited stories have dictated.

LEFT BRAIN-RIGHT BRAIN COMMUNICATION FOR BALANCE

1. Begin in a comfortable seat.

2. Clasp your hands together normally, fingers intertwined. Now reverse that clasp by making sure the opposite index finger and thumb are on top. This will likely feel awkward or strange. Keep your hands clasped this way during the breathing portion of the meditation, at which point you are free to unclasp afterwards if you like.

3. Breathe deeply for a few minutes.
    a. Notice how the breath feels entering in through the nose and going down the throat.
    b. Notice how your hands and fingers feel in this position.
    c. Notice how the chair supports your body.
    d. Notice how your bones get heavy.
    e. Notice the temperature on your skin.

4. Locate the center division line running from front to back in your skull, separating your two hemispheres.
    a. You might have a sensation.
    b. Perhaps you imagine this as a visual.
    c. Maybe you pretend this is happening.

5. Imagine that center division as an open highway with no limit to roads merging into it.
    a. Perhaps you imagine a large network of "on ramps" leading onto your highway from either side.
    b. Maybe you envision this highway more like a permeable canal with inlets.
    c. You might even imagine this to be a gentle, narrow pathway with many tiny off-shoots.

6. Imagine yourself on this road and the dark night sky represents the expanse of your brain. Imagine your dominant side of your brain being full of millions of stars made of your own neurons.
    a. Perhaps you see these stars twinkling.
    b. Maybe you imagine electrical activity in the night sky.
    c. Notice what sensations, thoughts, or images cross your mind.

7. Have those stars feed their light across the highway and through to the other side of your brain.
    a. Maybe the stars send twinkling light to each of the "on ramps" on your highway.
    b. Perhaps you imagine electrical current passing across the dividing line.

    c.   These may even appear as shooting stars racing from one side to the other.

    d.   Notice any thoughts or sensations that arise.

8.   Watch as the other side of your brain begins to reveal neural stars in its own night sky.

    a.   Perhaps you imagine stars in just one area of the sky at first.

    b.   Maybe your stars illuminate across the entire sky at once.

    c.   Notice how many stars you can create on this other side, compared to the side you started with.

9.   Have starlight or electric current run back and forth across the highway.

    a.   Play with how many stars light up on either side.

    b.   Notice any sensations or experiences this brings up.

10. Notice how you feel now as compared to before you began this exercise.

Make notes in your dedicated journal of any insights, sensations, thoughts, connections, or experiences.

Left Brain-Right Brain Communication for Enhanced Interoception

1.   Begin in a comfortable seat.

2.   Clasp your hands together normally, fingers intertwined. Now reverse that clasp by making sure the opposite index finger and thumb are on top. This will likely feel awkward or strange. Keep your hands clasped this way during the breathing portion of the meditation, at which point you are free to unclasp afterwards if you like.

3.   Breathe deeply for a few minutes.

    a.   Notice how the breath feels entering in through the nose and going down the throat.

    b.   Notice how your hands and fingers feel in this position.

    c.   Notice how the chair supports your body.

    d.   Notice how your bones get heavy.

    e.   Notice the temperature on your skin.

4.   Locate the center division line running from front to back in your skull, separating your two hemispheres.

    a.   You might have a sensation.

    b.   Perhaps you imagine this as a visual.

    c.   Maybe you pretend this is happening.

5.   Imagine that center division as an open highway with no limit to roads merging into it.

    a.   Perhaps you imagine a large network of "on ramps" leading onto your highway from either side.

    b.   Maybe you envision this highway more like a permeable canal.

    c.   You might even imagine this to be a gentle narrow pathway.

6.   Imagine yourself on this road, and the dark night sky represents the expanse of your brain. Imagine your dominant side of your brain being full of millions of stars made of your own neurons.

    a.   Perhaps you see these stars twinkling.

    b.   Maybe you imagine electrical activity in the night sky.

    c.   Notice what sensations, thoughts, or images cross your mind.

7.   Have those stars feed all of their light across the highway and through to the other side of your brain so that the first half is now black.

    a.   Maybe the stars send twinkling light to each of the "on ramps" on your highway.

    b.   Perhaps you imagine electrical current passing across the dividing line.

    c.   Notice any thoughts or sensations that arise.

8.   Watch as the other side of your brain begins to reveal neural stars in its own night sky.

    a.   Perhaps you imagine stars in just one area of the sky at first.

    b.   Maybe your stars illuminate across the entire sky at once.

    c.   Notice how many stars you can create on this other side compared to the side you started with.

9. Focus on quadrants of this new half of your night sky and have the stars in those quadrants grow as bright as they can
   a. Perhaps you envision the top of the sky lighting up first.
   b. Maybe you move on to the middle.
   c. Next you might imagine the bottom of the sky lighting up.
   d. You might even imagine smaller segments.
   e. Notice any experiences or sensations as this half of your brain contains all the stars.

10. Take a look at the first half of your brain in a completely black night sky.
    a. Notice what this brings up for you.

11. Slowly begin to draw starlight or electric current running back and forth across the highway, illuminating only the stars in the first half that represent **I AM** statements you are in resistance to.
    a. Discover how many stars in your night sky you have devoted to **I AM** statements you resist.
    b. Notice any sensations or experiences this brings up.

12. Once those stars are lit up, imagine them fizzling out across your night sky like shooting stars. These are no longer active stars.
    a. Notice your level of comfort with this step.

13. Continue to feed starlight or electric current back and forth until you feel the two halves of your night sky are balanced with about the same amount of twinkling stars.

14. Notice how you feel now as compared to before you began this exercise.

Make notes in your dedicated journal of any insights, sensations, thoughts, connections, or experiences.

Some of my clients experience this very viscerally. Those who prefer left-brain defaults noted that lighting up their right side gave them a profound sense of floating, colors got brighter, joy was accessible, and the relationship to the body changed. There were even some reports of individuals telling me they hadn't felt sensations like that without the use of chemicals or substance. Every person is different. Place value in your own experience with this exercise and allow yourself to observe what it does for you.

If you have a right-brain default, then lighting up your left side may feel totally different than anything I described here. Remember, the purpose of this exercise is to get you to look at and stimulate the side of your brain you are not defaulting to regularly. This communication normally happens through the center dividing line of the brain called the corpus callosum. You will notice different things as you darken one side and play with the amount of stars and brightness on each side. I've also played with a version of this exercise as a way to retrieve memories that weren't typically in my immediate recall. We all have our set of stories and memories we tell over and over—they only represent a fraction of what we've experienced. I began using this exercise to draw forth random memories I had totally forgotten about. Instead of separating the brain into two sides, I envisioned the entire brain as the nighttime sky. I'd start with the sky totally black. I'd relax deeply, then suddenly, with a burst of concentration, I'd imagine one small section of the sky lighting up and illuminating a random memory from an old and dusty memory file. Each time I did this, I unearthed mundane events I had totally forgotten about. This version was always fun for me. Feel free to use these exercises as your playground to help reveal to you new information and ways of interacting with your world.

Suggested Use:

Whenever you feel stuck in a mindset.

When you desire a completely different perspective.

Regularly as a balancing exercise.

Light up the right side when you desire a creative solution to a problem, insight, or a larger perspective.

Light up the left side when you desire analysis, logic application, or planning skills.

Chapter 15

EXERCISES FOR CHILDREN

"Example isn't another way to teach, it is the only way to teach."

~ Albert Einstein

I have found these techniques very helpful for children, but you must make your own decision about sharing these with your children. I will add a caveat here and emphasize that if you hope to teach these to your children, you must first use them yourself. Through your own use of them you will gain many insights into their subtleties and application, and you'll become a much better guide for your children.

Let's take a brief look at a child's brain. Up until the age of seven, most children function at a slower brain-wave frequency than the usual beta wave that corresponds to our adult alert waking state. Children are naturally closer to fantasy and dream space, as their brains are literally functioning there between a delta and theta wave frequency depending on their age. While some of the imagery in these exercises can be difficult for adults, children don't seem to have that problem. My daughter would often enhance the imagery with detailed side tracks and even parallel story lines at times. Her access to rich and colorful detail was, and still is, instantaneous. Children don't need to be taught to visualize; they only need to be encouraged to continue doing it.

EYES OF A CHILD

The limbic brain is a strong driver in children because the prefrontal cortex is in its infancy during those early years. This is why children expect instant gratification and must be taught patience. This is the same reason a child will engage in socially inappropriate behavior simply because it feels good. They have not yet developed strong abilities to inhibit socially unacceptable behavior because that attribute is regulated by the right frontal cortex. Remember, one of the ways in which we can control stress is through a healthy dialogue between the prefrontal cortex and the limbic brain. Children don't have this functionality the way adults do. Additionally, science is showing that all the prefrontal cortex needs to regulate the stress response is the *illusion* of control. So with my own daughter, I am of the mindset that if I give her a sense of control through her own stories, she may have a skill set to draw from during times of increased stress.

PLAY PRETEND

I began teaching my daughter these techniques as soon as she was old enough to ask me to tell her stories—probably around the age of three. I started with a fun and simple version of the grounding exercise. I began by telling her a make-believe story and asked her to envision her tail and its color. Children love stories, and more importantly, they love interacting with stories. There were times we drew pictures of her tail and gave it powers. I spent some time just getting her familiar with the story of it all before we used it with any purpose. She'd note how her tail felt, and sometimes she'd ask her friends about theirs. On the way home from daycare I'd ask her questions about her tail to encourage this open dialogue. There was never a moment's hesitation as her imagery was always vivid and accessible. Sometimes she'd tell me what color *my* tail was!

It was shortly after she witnessed me flatline that I realized I needed to address a level of trauma that neither I nor my daughter were prepared for. I'm guessing many parents do not prepare to address real mortality issues with their toddlers. To my great dismay, by the time my daughter was three we were having death conversations, rehearsing how to dial 911, practicing emergency scripts, and detailing what she should do for me until the paramedics showed up in the event it happened again. I had to teach her how to unlock the front door, which neighbors were safe to run to, which strangers were safe to let in, and many more logistics to which I had not given much thought prior to that day.

I was beginning to see that our experience shaped her view of permanence and security. No matter how strong she appeared, at a very young age she'd had the illusion of mommy's immortality erased forever. From my studies, I know that certainty and autonomy are wired into the brain as strongly as survival needs. I was aware that uncertainty could cause a stress response, while certainty and stability could cause a neurological reward response. Because of my education, I was acutely aware that a life rich with an anticipation of uncertainty and instability could lead to all sorts of neurological predispositions such as helplessness, depression, and even hypertension.

I believed these techniques could offer her a way to release the emotional charge associated with the imagery of that event and maybe ease the sting of pending uncertainty around it happening again. My studies and practice taught me that various stimuli associated with a fear response could be extricated, rewired, isolated, and neutralized.

We began using the grounding exercise before bed regularly to release any pictures, feelings, or images that might be bothering her. Sometimes she verbalized a sense of relief, but many times she simply seemed to enjoy playing along. We layered technique after technique until eventually she had many different methods she could use to address her fears or stress. Each night she'd put fearful or stressful images down her cord. She'd paint her cord with the color of safety. She'd clear out other children's words and influences from her bubble. She'd create positive associations with previously stressful events and stimuli. She'd simply relax.

There were other exercises we did that are not noted in this book, all of them intended to give her a sense of mastery over her stories and initiate a parasympathetic response. We used an entire regimen of techniques every night as part of her bedtime routine for at least three years. At that point, the exercises were so familiar to her that I felt that she could begin using them on her own, so I eased up on the bedtime routine and now simply ask her from time to time if she needs to use a tool or not. Sometimes she requests we do them together, and she notes her favorites.

She is very aware of her internal state for such a young child. She is a very articulate and empathic girl who often acts as the peacekeeper in social situations at school. I cannot say for sure what these exercises have done for her or continue to do for her. But I can say she loves them, returns to them as though they are old friends, and describes them to others when she sees someone in crisis. I have clients who play my CD for their children and note how much calmer they seem after using it. Additionally, I have workshops specifically for kids, and I have clients who bring their children in for private sessions.

You must trust your authority as a parent to decide how or if you want to share these with your child. I'd suggest evaluating these techniques yourself before trying to teach them to anyone else. You'll be a far better teacher of it if you are actually a practitioner as well!

CONSIDERATIONS

Keep it simple and fun.

Make it a bonding time between you and your child.

Let your child participate in this story time.

Ask your child questions like, "What does that feel like or look like?", "What colors make you feel happy?", "What kind of tail makes you think of strength?" It seems to work best if the child decides on the imagery. The only time I'd recommend suggesting a change to the child's story is if the specific imagery is causing any anxiety. By asking questions you can gently guide the child to more productive images.

If your child is very young, keep the "why" or "how" out of the exercise until they are old enough to understand an explanation—or inquisitive enough to ask for one.

If your child prefers to interact with the world through craft or action rather than story time, you can ask them to draw and color pictures of this imagery. This can be a very effective way to reach the same result.

Inquire about what your child experiences with these techniques and let them tell you. You may be surprised at their level of awareness. Remember, this is a lifelong practice, so you can take an easy pace when teaching this to children. As always, check with your pediatrician and mental health caregiver if you feel your child needs professional attention.

TEENAGERS

The buy-in for these techniques might be much more difficult with teenagers because by that age, their brains are culling their neural networks in an attempt to establish a concrete model of the world. In the early teenage years individuals can become more set in their thinking than small children. If it causes stress or anxiety to introduce these techniques to teenagers, you might want to rethink it. If your teenager is very stressed or misdirected, then do not use these techniques in lieu of professional medical advice. However, if your teenager is receptive to trying some of these, imagine what their awkward or turbulent years could be like with some of these navigation techniques. Imagine what *your* teenage years could have been like with some of these navigation techniques. Our teenagers' world is much more global and moves at a faster pace than even one generation earlier. Today we see a prevalence of neurological issues like ADD, ADHD, Autism, Asperger's Syndrome, and Obsessive Compulsive Disorder. The more we fill our youths' toolboxes, the better equipped they will be to handle the increasing demands our societies place on them.

PART III

LEARNING FROM THOSE WHO'VE GONE BEFORE US

REAL-LIFE EXAMPLES

"Insanity: doing the same thing over and over again and expecting different results."

~ Albert Einstein

My goal is to make this content as real and applicable for you as possible; otherwise, you might not be compelled to use it. I'm presenting three stories to you, from three very real clients of mine. Each case study varies in degree of stress and trauma. I've chosen to cover the spectrum from everyday stress to severe identity-crushing trauma in hopes that you will find yourself somewhere on this spectrum and know that you are not without hope in mastering your stress. The common thread with each of these individuals is that they recognized their consistent approach to life was not working. Each of these individuals represents the courage and willingness to open to alternative solutions and a new way to navigate their lives. I invite you now to meet some amazing and brave individuals.

Chapter 16

SAM

Sam was a high-school social studies teacher in an inner-city school district. He coached the policy debate team, was committed to his job, and seemed extremely enthusiastic when he first came to me. However, inside he was burnt out, frustrated, angry, and having an increasingly difficult time managing his stress well. Sam had many years of experience meditating, having begun his own practice at age nineteen. Although he grew up in a rural and conservative family, he was compelled to seek more alternative methods of inward reflection than those he grew up with. Even with almost ten years of meditation under his belt, he felt ill-prepared to cope well with working in an inner-city school whose infrastructure was being rebuilt from the ground up. The environment was turbulent and volatile. Sam's health routine suffered, as he became overworked and had less and less time and motivation to take care of himself at home. He felt as though he were treading water to operate in a classroom.

Sam's perception was that the onus of educating the children fell entirely on his shoulders. As a pillar, he was cracking. His meditation practice had suffered and was now only a sporadic luxury he squeezed in from time to time between his 5:30 a.m. wake-up and 7 p.m. clock-out-of-work schedule. His busy and frustrating days left little to no sense of accomplishment. Interactions with students, coworkers, and friends suffered. He found himself drinking more so he could get numb.

He began to engage in dysfunctional power struggles with his students. He felt the meditation practice he cultivated wasn't practical in this real-time context. Quieting his mind seemed to have little application or opportunity in his day-to-day existence. In his relationship with meditation, as I find with many who come to me, he felt that in order to do it, he needed to remove himself from the world, walk off into the woods for days, or sit high up on some mountaintop to attain peace. He felt that his meditation sometimes even removed him socially or made him more distant at work. He felt his advancement in meditation necessitated the end of his career.

As a meditation practitioner, I understood his dilemma. I, too, have enjoyed many amazing practices that necessitated silent retreat or social isolation. These are not the techniques I teach for use in everyday life precisely because of the frustration it created for Sam.

I taught Sam four of the techniques presented in this book: grounding, neutral space, personal boundary, and gold sun. Additionally, over the years, I have taught him some others he uses regularly. He was an amazingly apt practitioner, integrating the methods immediately into his daily life. He simply was ready for a change. Sam noted that instead of attaining a high, spiritual, far-away state he could reconnect to the present moment by clearing thoughts and patterns out of his space. For Sam, the grounding cord changed everything.

He was particularly fond of both the grounding and gold sun techniques. He used them in the morning and as a check-in during the day to see if he was moving things. Rather than trying to conceptually annihilate the ego and find calm, he loved filling up with the things he wanted to emanate in the world. Sam called it his "spiritual morning smoothie."

The benefits were fast and blatant. He noticed immediate changes in the classroom. He reported that since he was no longer full of ill-serving thoughts and patterns, he noticed his own contribution to life's daily drama. He was able to mitigate half the intensity immediately. He noticed fewer power struggles with students—which, at an inner-city school, is quite an accomplishment. He described it to me this way: Prior to using these techniques he'd bring his full cup to the table, spill some, and get into it with the students.

Sam quickly found real-time application and was able to ground immediately during heated confrontation. He noticed it profoundly defused situations, as there was no longer a target for the students to swing at. Like dissipating trails of smoke, his fading anger and frustration left them nothing to engage with. Sam called it "true magic." His leadership abilities increased as well. He found an enhanced ability to hold space for students who were upset—used grounding during intense emotional downloads from students. He was able to step out of a space of trying to fix them, and instead, he showed them empathy and real support. He attributes his ability to the grounding exercise.

It changed his relationship with coworkers, as well. He began to ground before meetings in a heated environment. Previously, Sam was considered overly vocal in meetings—even confrontational. After using the methods for just a short time he articulated a new ability to discern the value of when his comments would forward a situation versus damage it. Coworkers noticed changes and some began to ask about his process. I eventually led some training sessions for numerous teachers in his school.

During the year, he continued to identify new benefits of the exercises—always excited to share his growth with me. He told me grounding cleared out his past, while the gold sun recreated the present. He'd cycle daily between clearing and filling in. He often imagined the gold sun to be on time-release so he could enjoy an intentional state all day long. His relationships with students continued to improve. He called the gold sun his chewing device. Whatever intention he put in there became a baseline against which he'd juxtapose his thoughts at any moment and chew on them for a while until he noticed either alignment or incongruences. He was empowered.

Sam's previous meditation practice felt akin to the neutral-space exercise, so he chose not to focus on that one. As he found his preferences, so will you. No longer restricted to only meditating at the end of the school year when he could retreat into the woods, he was successfully navigating mindfully in the here and now. Sam noted that since learning these techniques, he was able to find solace and peace of mind in the inner-city where he lives. No longer functioning on finite reserves, he thrived by regenerating his positive beliefs everyday. The benefits of this alone are a mile long.

Sam was experiencing a new ability to stay neutral and not take professional systemic changes personally. He was no longer losing sleep or anesthetizing after work. He gained productivity even after coming to work later in the morning and leaving earlier at night. He was no longer taking stress and work home with him, and he noted having more breakthroughs with students, parents, and coworkers. He told me he finally felt like he was a positive cause in matters and not the effect. He was no longer intimidated by others with status, and he spoke more articulately on matters from a neutral perspective.

Years later, he credits these tools as the foundation for his deeper work facilitating leadership and transformational programs for teenagers. Recently, he noted that these techniques enabled him to remain calm, productive, and completely available for the thirty-six American students he took to Kenya for about a month. He attributed much of his growth and success to what he called this real-time meditation.

Even though Sam's story wasn't full of trauma, his transformation through daily practice was profound.

Chapter 17

OFFICERS' EVERYDAY TRAUMA

We expect and hope police officers are stable, strong, well-adjusted, full of integrity, and able to approach situations with neutrality, fairness, and skill. The truth is that officers in this country are trained well in tactical skills and very poorly in emotional regulation. This imbalance has caused an epidemic about which I am very passionate. When one in three officers suffers PTSD, and more commit suicide every year than die in the line of duty, then we all have a big problem. And this is exactly the reality in this country. You may not be an officer or even know anyone personally in law enforcement, but I urge you to pay attention to both Joseph's and Kathy's stories. They are great examples of the hidden reality behind the badge, and they will prepare you with a greater understanding the next time you encounter an officer.

Joseph's Story

Joseph is one of my law-enforcement clients. I label him this way so you can immediately understand that his level of traumatic exposure may exceed what's considered normal. On a daily basis, officers are potentially exposed to theft, domestic abuse, drug violence, weapons assault, crimes against children, drug and human trafficking, homicide, and suicide. If your stress level is manageable then you may not associate with his situation—however, you can find an appreciation for the power of these techniques as you learn more about Joseph. If your level of trauma is as great as his, you may find a light at the end of the tunnel.

Joseph e-mailed me one day, having heard of my work with law-enforcement agencies. He requested a private consultation. When I spoke with him on the phone, he told me he was at his edge. He felt he couldn't get help from inside his own police agency, nor did he feel encouraged, supported, or safe enough to use the confidential counseling services his agency offered. I reiterated to Joseph that what I could assist him with was not counseling, but learning a meditation practice. He noted he was ready for that. I have found this to be an extremely unfortunate and common perception of counseling services in that industry. Even though officers are told it's confidential, most of them will not take advantage of the psychiatric support available as they feel it may stigmatize them, brand them as weak, and put their job security and integrity at risk. Unfortunately, officers don't get the help they need, and some of them end up suffering horrible consequences.

To combat this, there's a growing trend in agencies to create peer-support groups. These individuals usually receive extra training and act as the go-to person for their peers in crisis. My experience has shown that the peer-support officers work double duty, performing all the tasks of a normal officer before sacrificing off-duty hours to assist their peers during intense crisis. For these individuals, their work trauma doubles.

Joseph is one of the lucky officers who was able to detect a downward spiral *before* it completely destroyed him. He relayed the details of a fairly recent call he'd gone on.

He was at a homicide scene: dead man on the floor, brains and blood leaking out of his head. The dead man's wife was off to the side, in shock and bearing witness to her husband's lifeless body as police stepped over and around his corpse as though he were furniture. Joseph emphasized to me that this type of thing didn't faze him at all. This is simply part of his day. His responsibilities at the scene were winding down. He recalled walking over the dead man's body, looking at the stunned wife, then calling his fellow officers to find out where everyone was meeting for lunch. He, like most officers, was skilled at instantly switching gears. It was no effort to go to lunch with a hearty appetite and socialize with peers. Yet he noticed he was becoming very irritable at home, and he was easily triggered by seemingly inconsequential things like a commercial or a television show. He mentioned television shows could bring him to tears or send him into a rage very easily.

He told me that he felt his life was backwards, and he was beginning to become frightened of his ability to desensitize to horrific trauma yet become reactionary to everyday matters. He was on edge all the time, and it was getting in the way of his happiness, his relationship with his wife and son, and his ability to understand his own behavior. Additionally, since he was in the canine unit, his partner was a trained canine who not only shared his day, but went home with him at night. For Joseph, there was never an opportunity to leave work at the office as he was the caregiver of the only partner he worked with. An officer's day can be very isolated as they patrol individually, or sometimes in pairs, but never in teams as firefighters do. This isolation compounds any stress or trauma an officer experiences.

At our first appointment, he mentioned he'd gained a large amount of weight over the last year and hadn't been exercising. The weight gain and lack of physical motivation was bothering him. He couldn't remember the last time he slept through the night. For a very long time, he'd only slept in three-hour chunks, most of them interrupted by brief moments of waking or needing to use the bathroom. By my estimation, Joseph looked to be in his mid-thirties. What he was describing to me is commonly representative of most of the officers I deal with. Many officers begin their careers in great physical shape but quickly slip into sub-prime condition, become sleep-deprived, desensitized, de-motivated, overweight, angry, and confused.

Joseph confided that since he hung up the phone after our initial discussion, he'd broken down in tears and hadn't stopped crying for days. While some of you reading this may not find that remarkable, I can tell you from working with law-enforcement trauma that it is quite remarkable when an officer can cry. It's a complete and total moment of vulnerability—precisely the thing they fight hard to conceal and exactly the thing they might need to do in order to heal. He welled up with tears in my office as he continued to tell me how he'd watched the vibrant life he once had slip away. I have found many officers share the same sentiment as they tell me their lives are not what they had wanted them to be. He mentioned that his young son was his primary anchor. Because what I do doesn't involve counseling, I didn't need for Joseph to dive in to any personal details he wasn't comfortable sharing. He told me he was ready for help, any sort of help, and that he was open to try anything.

He spent most of our first session learning and practicing the grounding technique to my guided instructions. Immediately as he grounded, his body began to twitch. His pectoral muscles and biceps twitched rapidly as I asked him to envision stress in his chest melting away. He had finger and leg tremors, as well. Remember, often during a parasympathetic response one can experience tremors and shaking, just like animals in the wild as they dissipate their adrenaline. Tears came freely for him again during the release process.

Just after the exercise, he told me he hadn't felt that way in years. I saw a very profound change in his face, mostly in his eyes. When he first walked into my office, his eyes were desperate and searching, but they were wide and hopeful when he walked out. In our next session, we did a version of the brain synchrony exercise. As Joseph lit up the left side of his brain, nothing seemed to shift, as I suspect that's a place where he was comfortable. As he activated the right side of his brain I noticed quite a different expression take over his face. He relaxed, his coloring became more vibrant, and the corners of his mouth turned up into a slight smirk. After the exercise he was very excited to tell me that activating his right brain amplified all the colors in his visualization, and that he felt a profound sense of floating and lightness. He noted he hadn't felt that for years and seemed very animated and excited by the experience. He mentioned that using this exercise seemed like a way for him to tap into his creativity and relate to his son, to whom he desperately wanted to stay connected. He was even more hopeful after this session than the first and mentioned that he was urging his own mother, a psychologist, to learn some of these techniques.

After just the first two sessions, Joseph reported he was sleeping a full night's sleep for the first time in years. He was using **Name It and Tame It** regularly, and he noticed an instant drop in stress intensity when he did. While his stress is still something he's learning how to navigate, he has become much more aware of his triggers, of his choices in those moments, and of his own ability to win over that insidious cycle.

KATHY'S STORY

Kathy was a hostage negotiator and peer-support officer during the time I was teaching her these techniques. She is no longer an officer. Kathy's mother contacted me some years ago after hearing about what I do. She asked if I would work with her daughter—an out-of-state officer in a high-profile city and agency. My first conversation with Kathy revealed what, unfortunately, *really* goes on inside certain agencies.

She was a good cop with strong ethics and a real desire for fairness. After an exemplary career, she committed the ultimate industry sin: She turned in a fellow officer for wrong doing. If you're not in law enforcement, you might expect this was a good thing to do, as she deemed this officer's behavior was unethical. In fact, during all of her job interviews in various police departments, a key question presented to her was, "If you see an officer committing a crime what do you do?" The correct and expected answer is to tell the officer personally that you know she did something wrong and offer to go with her to turn herself in, or *you* will have to turn her in. Reality isn't quite like that. An act like this is viewed very differently on the inside. There is a prevalent code of silence in this country's police industry; it's called the "thin blue line." According to this code it's practically the kiss of death to turn in a fellow officer for wrongdoing. You are considered a snitch, the lowest possible life form, untrustworthy, and no longer part of the "brotherhood." And there are serious consequences for that. Michael Quinn reveals much about this code in his controversial book *Walking With the Devil: The Police Code of Silence*.

Kathy walked with the devil.

Once she turned in her fellow officer, she instantly had a false internal affairs counter-investigation launched against her. Individuals broke into her locker several times, jamming broken keys in the lock. Someone ran her personal information through the state and federal information system (NCIC) to find her address. Then her home mailbox was broken into. Someone tampered with her payroll, broke into her home, and punched holes in the badge of her business card on her locker—suggesting death to an officer, according to the code of silence. She was verbally harassed by a top union member while out in public at dinner: He wanted her to turn over evidence so the union wouldn't get in trouble. Individuals mailed letters to all the city council members, the mayor, and several members of the police department noting that Kathy was an alcoholic, a drug user, and a variety of other things. She had over a year's worth of internal-affairs interrogations, court appearances, and hostile work environment to deal with. Her health failed, she was in chronic pain, breaking out in hives, and in a constant state of stress and fear. She had been in and out of the hospital for what seemed like stress-related issues.

This was Kathy's story when I first began working with her.

I worked with her for nine months. Our sessions were all done over the phone, as she lived out of state. I taught her all of the techniques in this book, plus many others. The sessions involved a discussion about the benefits of each technique, a guided walkthrough of the exercise, and then a discussion period regarding how she could use these, when, and what she might expect to experience. The goal was to first get her able to calm down her own stress response and help her body move out of chronic pain. Once that process seemed well on its way, I began teaching her exercises to help her stay neutral and out of her limbic brain during her court appearances. She reported that this enabled her to remain articulate, calm, and grounded during these sessions. Additionally, I taught her derivatives of the personal boundary exercise so she could separate herself from the hostile work environment in which she was immersed every day.

What happens to many officers after retirement is commonly viewed as an identity crisis because they don't just work as cops, they *are* cops. They view this as their identity. Another angle we took was to practice techniques in which, through her own interoception, she could begin to define who she was versus what she did for a living. At that point, even if she made it through her ordeal intact, she'd likely have to deal with the identity crisis waiting for her after her police career.

Kathy took the practice seriously, as she had already been through some other types of trainings and knew this was likely her last resort. She practiced the techniques and made time for regular training sessions with me. After nine months of training, Kathy successfully navigated her career and life falling apart. She is now back in school pursuing a career she feels she can stand behind. She credits the techniques as saving her marriage and health through that process.

A recent update from Kathy noted some amazing repercussions from her experience. She notes that the techniques helped her differentiate that being a cop was her job and not her identity. One of her fellow officers who knew the truth of the corruption and who had urged her not to snitch later found himself in a situation where he had to turn another officer in. Finally, a coworker who could empathize with her predicament! He has since apologized to Kathy, commending her for her bravery because he now knows how difficult that is. One of the captains Kathy was forced to deal with has since filed a hostile work environment case against the department. Additionally, the sergeant who continually wrote up Kathy for a slew of invented incidents has since apologized to her for the way he treated her.

Kathy's story is one of strong personal and professional victory. She navigated her intense fear and threat cycle during a very real time of danger—unlike the perceived danger many of us deal with in our day-to-day lives. While wearing the uniform might have made Kathy feel like a warrior, it was navigating her intense experience and coming out okay on the other side that proved to her she was stronger than she knew. Most importantly, she realized throughout the process that her perception of these events was a choice. Instead of choosing defeat, she chose victory and rewrote her identity and story.

"Wisdom is not a product of schooling but of the lifelong attempt to acquire it."

~ Albert Einstein

Chapter 18

THE MAP

By now, if you've done the exercises, you've had quite a journey! Congratulations on diving in deep to your own ability to access information and begin rewriting your own stories. The journey looked something like this.

THE RE-TELL

You learned that you carry old stories with you, created at a point in time long ago, which whisper incessantly, causing you to respond to limited and outdated beliefs. These stories speak up at inconvenient and opportunistic moments, creating reactions that are not representative of the present moment. The voice of these stories is the end result of an ongoing negotiation between many different parts of the brain. You know that your stories, pieces of which are partially invented by your mind, create your history and a projection of who you are in the world. The stories that carry a negative charge prime you to identify similar negativity in the world. Since this is an energy-efficient default option for your brain, it's far easier to believe those negative stories. This cyclical pattern results in compromised mental, physical, emotional, and spiritual health. This state of being then perpetuates itself in your life and in those around you.

Having a healthy dialogue between the left and right brain is the key to balancing the fabrication and the reality of your stories. You know that your brain is much more plastic and elastic than it is firm and inflexible. Our own neural growth and regeneration is much more easily influenced than we even suspected just fifty years ago. Having a strong and healthy prefrontal cortex can mitigate and even override a threat response from the limbic brain. Through intention and daily practice each of us has the ability to consciously participate in the process of remapping. Down-regulating emotional responses, hormones, and our fight-or-flight response is an integral piece of mastering that process.

You cannot effectively change external situations or anyone else until you clean up your own internal chaos, fear, and stress. Vast healing and information regarding a new set of stories also lives in your brain. These positive stories have the power to create new neural pathways encoded to override some of those negative default options. Telling these new stories in the right context, even once, begins that process. You learned that even deep trauma can be a signpost indicating a hidden path towards healing.

You were introduced to six powerful techniques as part of a lifelong regimen, each of which can be used for varying degrees of interoception and healing.

Grounding:

This begins a parasympathetic response in your body and encourages the nervous system to associate that response with being in the here and now. It helps you separate from emotional charge and down-regulate the limbic brain's fight-or-flight cycle. It can be used to discover information regarding patterns and cycles contributing to your daily stress.

Neutrality:

The neutrality exercise helps you look at situations outside of your biases, as a way to gain more relevant information and detach from a default emotional response. It enables you to see the gorilla in the middle of the basketball game. It enhances a perspective no longer connected to threat or error-detection mode. It also contributes to the strengthening of the prefrontal cortex. This exercise can be used to gain insight and clarity regarding emotionally charged situations and memories.

Personal Boundaries:

You experienced that others' influences can impact your own sense of personal space and add to the confusion of your stories. This exercise enables you to remain open and socially connected, while gaining an awareness of how those social interactions affect your moods, biases, worldview, and decisions. This practice can be helpful in learning how to identify your true values versus those that are logistically or environmentally influenced. This also enables you to separate work and home life in order to find balance and integrity in each.

Filling In:

This exercise allows you to stamp a new mindset with a conscious intention as a way to participate in the recreation of these old patterns. It offers a reference point against which you can examine troublesome situations or your own uncomfortable and painful perspectives. It offers the opportunity to come back to zero, start over, and recalibrate.

Cleansing and Programming:

You practiced a simple reprogramming technique that can be an effective way to combine relaxation states and prefrontal cortex learning. Regular use of this exercise can help encode new learning paths with usable and relevant content. It offers one a sense of self-direction, goal-setting, motivation, and autonomy.

Left Brain–Right Brain Communication:

Finally, you began the identification and dialogue between the stories that live in the left and right sides of the brain. Through this exercise you can experiment with your comfort zones and learn a great deal about how to bring a more holistic approach to your own life participation. This exercise can be used to gain insight into your relationship with the social world around you.

YOU ARE HERE

Congratulations! On the map that leads you to freedom from stress and fear, you've arrived at the starting point designated by the *You Are Here* sign. You've jumped onto the path with momentum. From this point forward, for the rest of your life, you will *always* be on the map, even during times you get distracted and veer away from your journey. It is a continuing process which often includes getting lost and finding your way again. I view these techniques as the compass. You may not use them every day, in each moment, but once you've realized you've lost your way, you can reach in to your pocket and pull out the compass to steer you back to your path. The good news is you don't have to start from the beginning each time you lose your way; you simply jump back onto the path at the point of your distraction and let your tools guide you onward. There's no need for judgment, disappointment, or thoughts of failure, as the journey doesn't have any external time limits. It simply lasts your entire life.

These techniques are not the pot of gold at the end of the rainbow; this process offers treasures all along your path from start to finish. Some of those treasures are small tokens reminding you that you're do- ing a good job, while others are huge, life-changing shifts. The riches and abundance inherent in your being are there for the taking. Once you give yourself permission to heal without the hammer of your own judgment, your life becomes a wondrous journey.

Each trauma or stumbling point is an opportunity for growth, learn- ing, and forgiveness. The more you commit to this course of healing, the more apparent those opportunities become. Fear and stress don't disap- pear completely from your life; instead they show up more like diversions or speed bumps rather than foreboding walls or fatal accidents.

Our brains are wired to prefer predictability and certainty over instabil- ity and uncertainty. Each time we encounter the unknown we need extra resources, patience, and compassion to navigate without defaulting to fear. While the brain prefers predictability, the one thing it can ironically predict is that nothing is truly predictable! As humans we have the task of experiencing this dichotomy with as much pain or grace as we decide. It is a choice.

I value the time you've invested in reading this book, and I value the journey on which you've embarked. This journey is my life's mission, and I'm not content to let you close these pages without offering a few last thoughts to ponder as you continue with your life.

Where in your life are you continuing to play the victim?

Where in your life do you default to projecting the worst-case scenario?

Where in your life do you believe it's too good to be true?

Where in your life have you short-changed your abilities?

Where in your life do you believe you deserve anything less than the best?

What resources do you have to change all of this?

You know your own answers. I wish for you to use these answers in your continuing meditation practice as you free yourself from stress and fear.

You are not alone.

You are in good company.

You are entirely capable.

You deserve grace.

BIBLIOGRAPHY

Bolte Taylor, Jill. *My Stroke of Insight.* (New York: Viking, 2006), 32-33.

Bishop, Scott, Mark Lau, Shauna Shapiro, Linda Carlson, Nicole D. Anderson, James Carmody, Zindel V. Segal, Susan Abbey, Michael Speca, Drew Velting, and Gerald Devins. *Mindfulness: A Proposed Operational Definition.* (American Psychological Association, 2004).

Castanada, Carlos. *The Teachings of Don Juan: A Yaqui Way of Knowledge.* (California: University of California Press, 1968).

Collier, Azurii, and Dr. Mark Jung-Beeman and Dr. John Kounios. *How Insight Happens: Learning From the Brain.* (Neuroleadership Journal, 2008).

Covey, Stephen R. *The Seven Habits of Highly Effective People.* (New York: Free Press, 1989).

Davachi, Lila, and Ian G. Dobbins. *Declarative Memory.* (Association for Psychological Science: NYU and Washington University, 2008).

Eagleman, David. *Incognito: The Secret Lives of the Brain.* (US: Pantheon, UK: Canongate, 2011).

Franken, Al. *Stuart Smalley. Saturday Night Live.* (New York: 1991).

Gilmartin, Kevin. *Emotional Survival for Law Enforcement.* (Arizona: E-S Press, 1999).

Levine, Peter. *Waking the Tiger: Healing Trauma.* (North Atlantic Books, 1997).

Lipton, Bruce H. *The Biology of Belief: Unleashing the Power of Consciousness, Matter & Miracles.* (California: Hay House Inc., 2011).

Lorayne, Harry. *How to Develop a Super Power Memory.* (New American Library, 1958).

Lorayne, Harry. *Harry Lorayne's Secrets of Mind Power.* (1961).

Northrup, Christiane. *Women's Bodies, Women's Wisdom: Creating Physical and Emotional Health and Healing.* (New York: Bantam Books, 1994).

Perlmutter, David, and Alberto Villoldo. *Power Up Your Brain: The Neuroscience of Enlightenment.* (California: Hay House Inc., 2011).

Quinn, Michael. *Walking With the Devil: The Police Code of Silence.* (Quinn and Associates: 2005).

Watts, Alan. *The Book: On the Taboo Against Knowing Who You Are.* (Vintage, 1966).

Wilber, Ken. *The Holographic Paradigm and Other Paradoxes.* (Colorado: Shambhala Publications Inc, 1982).

Wills, Christopher. *The Runaway Brain: The Evolution of Human Uniqueness.* (London: HarperCollins Publisher, 1993).

Wimberger, Lisa. "The Girl with Curious Eyes." (*Deathrealm Magazine,* 1991).

ABOUT THE AUTHOR

LISA WIMBERGER holds a masters degree in education from the University of Stonybrook, NY, and a Foundations Certification in NeuroLeadership. She is the founder of the Neurosculpting® Institute, Ripple Effect, LLC, and The Trance Personnel Consulting Group. Lisa has created and facilitated leadership trainings for executive teams in Fortune 500 companies, the Colorado Department of Health Care Policy and Finance, and worked individually with international management. She has created and facilitated emotional survival programs for law enforcement agencies and peer counsel groups. Lisa writes for CopsAlive, *The Elephant Journal,* and Safe Call Now, and partners with the Law Enforcement Survival Institute. Lisa is a member of the National Center for Crisis Management and International Law Enforcement Educators and Trainers Association (ILEETA).

Lisa is a private meditation teacher and psychic practitioner applying over thirty years of meditation experience. She is also a certified MBTI consultant, teaching clients who suffer stress disorders. Lisa studied Ascension training for four years with Ishaya monks. She completed two and a half years of psychic awareness training at ICI, applying the tools of the Berkeley Psychic Institute, and an additional year and a half of postgraduate studies. She currently has an international private practice, runs the institute, teaches workshops, and lectures.

Lisa has a parallel career as an international tribal percussionist in multiple bands with her husband, Gilly Gonzalez. Lisa's training in West African and Afro Cuban rhythms create a modern improvisational foundation for performance art, multiple movie scores, and domestic and international music projects.

CONTACT PAGE

To book Lisa for lectures, workshops, or private sessions contact:

info@neurosculptinginstitute.com

www.neurosculptinginstitute.com
www.newbeliefsnewbrain.com
www.tpconsultinggroup.com

Visit www.neurosculptinginstitute.com to find out about downloadable audio programs and recordings, articles, resources, and information regarding upcoming workshops in your city.

HERE ARE OTHER **DIVINE ARTS** BOOKS YOU MAY ENJOY

THE SACRED SITES OF THE DALAI LAMAS
by Glenn H. Mullin

"As this most beautiful book reveals, the Dalai Lamas continue to teach us that there are, indeed, other ways of thinking, other ways of being, other ways of orienting ourselves in social, spiritual, and ecological space."

— Wade Davis, Explorer-in-Residence, National Geographic Society

THE SHAMAN & AYAHUASCA: *Journeys to Sacred Realms*
by Don José Campos

"This remarkable and beautiful book suggests a path back to understanding the profound healing and spiritual powers that are here for us in the plant world. This extraordinary book shows a way toward reawakening our respect for the natural world, and thus for ourselves."

— John Robbins, author, *The Food Revolution* and *Diet for a New America*

LISTEN TO THE WIND, SPEAK FROM THE HEART
by Roger Thunderhands Gilbert

Roger Thunderhands Gilbert shares how he listens to the inner/higher spirit in himself and in all things. He speaks from the heart, passing on the wisdom of Spirit in plain, understandable, and passionate language. Combining shamanistic and Eastern knowledge, healing techniques, and practices, this book delivers an important synthesis of insights needed in today's global culture.

A HEART BLOWN OPEN:
The Life & Practice of Zen Master Jun Po Denis Kelly Roshi
by Keith Martin-Smith

"This is the story of our time... an absolute must-read for anyone with even a passing interest in human evolution..."

— Ken Wilber, author, *Integral Spirituality*

"This is the legendary story of an inspiring teacher that mirrors the journey of many contemporary Western seekers."

— Alex Grey, artist and author of *Transfigurations*

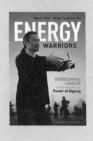

ENERGY WARRIORS
Overcoming Cancer and Crisis with the Power of Qigong
by Bob Ellal and Lawrence Tan

Energy Warriors learn to draw on something deeper during crisis. Using the clarity that comes when you use the ancient Chinese art and science of Qigong, four-time cancer survivor Bob Ellal shares his experiences of healing while Master Lawrence Tan presents a compelling and informative introduction to Qigong.

YEAR ZERO: *Time of the Great Shift*

by Kiara Windrider

"I can barely contain myself as I implode with gratitude for the gift of *Year Zero*! Every word resonates on a cellular level, awakening ancient memories and realigning my consciousness with an unshakable knowing that the best has yet to come. This is more than a book; it is a manual for building the new world!"

　　— Mikki Willis, founder, ELEVATE

ILAHINOOR: *Awakening the Divine Human*

by Kiara Windrider

"Ilahinoor is a truly precious and powerful gift for those yearning to receive and integrate Kiara Windrider's guidance on their journey for spiritual awakening and wisdom surrounding the planet's shifting process."

　　— Alexandra Delis-Abrams, Ph.D., author *Attitudes, Beliefs, and Choices*

THE MESSAGE: *A Guide to Being Human*

by LD Thompson

"Simple, profound, and moving! The author has been given a gift... a beautiful way to distill the essence of life into an easy-to-read set of truths, with wonderful examples along the way. Listen... for that is how it all starts."

　　— Lee Carroll, author, the *Kryon* series; co-author, *The Indigo Children*

SOPHIA—THE FEMININE FACE OF GOD:
Nine Heart Paths to Healing and Abundance

by Karen Speerstra

"Karen Speerstra shows us most compellingly that when we open our hearts, we discover the wisdom of the Feminine all around us. A totally refreshing exploration, and beautifully researched read."

　　— Michael Cecil, author, *Living at the Heart of Creation*

A FULLER VIEW: *Buckminster Fuller's Vision of Hope and Abundance for All*

by L. Steven Sieden

"This book elucidates Buckminster Fuller's thinking, honors his spirit, and creates an enthusiasm for continuing his work."

　　— Marianne Williamson, author, *Return To Love* and *Healing the Soul of America*

GAIA CALLS: *South Sea Voices, Dolphins, Sharks & Rainforests*

by Wade Daok

"Wade has the soul of a dolphin, and has spent a life on and under the oceans on a quest for deep knowledge. This is an important book that will change our views of the ocean and our human purpose."

　　— Ric O'Barry, author, *Behind the Dolphin Smile* and star of *The Cove,* which won the 2010 Academy Award for Best Documentary

1.800.833.5738 • 25% discount available online • www.divineartsmedia.com

DIVINE
ARTS

DIVINE ARTS sprang to life fully formed as an intention to bring spiritual practice into daily living. Human beings are far more than the one-dimensional creatures perceived by most of humanity and held static in consensus reality. There is a deep and vast body of knowledge — both ancient and emerging — that informs and gives us the understanding, through direct experience, that we are magnificent creatures occupying many dimensions with untold powers and connectedness to all that is. Divine Arts books and films explore these realms, powers and teachings through inspiring, informative and empowering works by pioneers, artists and great teachers from all the wisdom traditions.

We invite your participation and look forward to learning how we may better serve you.

Onward and upward,

Michael Wiese
Publisher/Filmmaker

DivineArtsMedia.com